George Washington Wagenseller

The History of the Wagenseller Family in America

With kindred branches

George Washington Wagenseller

The History of the Wagenseller Family in America
With kindred branches

ISBN/EAN: 9783337385866

Printed in Europe, USA, Canada, Australia, Japan

Cover: Foto ©ninafisch / pixelio.de

More available books at **www.hansebooks.com**

THE HISTORY

OF THE

WAGENSELLER FAMILY IN AMERICA,

With Kindred Branches.

Edited and Compiled by
GEO. W. WAGENSELLER, A. M.,
Middleburgh, Pa.

"Those who do not look upon themselves as a link connecting the past with
the future do not perform their duty to the world."—DANIEL WEBSTER.

MIDDLEBURGH, PENNA.:
WAGENSELLER PUBLISHING COMPANY.

1898.

PREFACE.

In presenting this volume of family history to the public and especially to those most interested in its contents, the author feels a great pleasure, but mingled with this he finds a strong under current of regret. The data long ere this should have been collected and preserved. Now, alas! we know not how much has been lost. The information now obtainable concerning the revered founder of our family in America is very meagre, but we still hope that time and research will yet reveal some important information so much coveted. The argument was used by some of our good friends that the publication of this volume should be delayed in order to secure more time and hence additional opportunity to make further research. This idea is a good one, but in order to get the book published, it was necessary not only for the author to contribute his services, but to select a time and opportunity to publish the book at a minimum cost in order to avoid the unfortunate condition of a losing venture, which, even with the strictest economy, is not yet assured. With all this the author was compelled to rob his business of much valuable time in order to accomplish this result. Hence, any additional delay would militate too much upon time that requires a more substantial reward. It is a pleasure, then, that so much has been accomplished, but a regret that so much must be left unearthed.

The appearance of this volume, at this time, must not be misconstrued to mean that no additional research shall be made, but on the other hand, putting the information already collected into the hands of those most interested, all will be in a better position to make research and notes upon all connecting lines, jot them down upon the blank pages in the back part of the book in order to preserve them. The time will come sooner or later when such information can be used. If any errors have occurred, and we know there have, for it is an impossibility to handle so many dates without errors, also note these upon the blank pages and report them at once to the undersigned.

In our work we have had the co-operation of a great many different persons who faithfully did their share of the work and to all of them we acknowledge our sincere gratitude for their devotion and loyalty to the preservation of the family records. We desire especially to acknowledge in grateful remembrance the invaluable services of Mrs. M. H. Hazzard of West Chester, Pa.; Hon. A. B. Longaker, Norristown, Pa.; Mr. William Summers, Conshohocken, Pa. and to Mr. Henry S. Dotterer, 1305 North Thirteenth Street, Philadelphia, who is the author of the "Perkiomen Region," a bound volume treating largely of the original Wagenseller locality, from whose pages we drew a great deal of data. There are many others who deserve special mention here, but space forbids. There is another class, and one entirely too large, who have neglected to answer even a single letter. It is this class who have erected barriers to the speedy and effectual disposition of a labor of love.

In the compilation of this work, after examining a number of different systems, we have adopted the one in use as the most popular and the one most easily followed. Every character is numbered and whenever one of them is to be taken up later for a more complete consideration, a plus (+) mark is prefixed to the number. The exponents are used to designate the generations to which a character belongs, thus, WILLIAM³, (*John²*, *Christopher¹*,) p. 37, indicates that William belongs to the third generation; John, his father, to the second, and Christopher, his grand-father to the first generation. The frontispiece represents the headstones at the graves of John and Margaret Wagenseller in the Old Trappe burying-ground in Montgomery County, Pa. Those who are not familiar with the German, will find a free translation of the inscriptions on page 19. In the back part of the book, page 209, will be found a picture of the POST PRINTING OFFICE, where this history was published.

With this introduction we submit this volume to the interested reader asking for lenient criticism for errors and that censure for deficiencies be placed where they properly belong.

Respectfully submitted,

Geo. W. Wagenseller

Middleburgh, Pa.,
    August, 1898.

Wagenseller Chart for Four Generations.

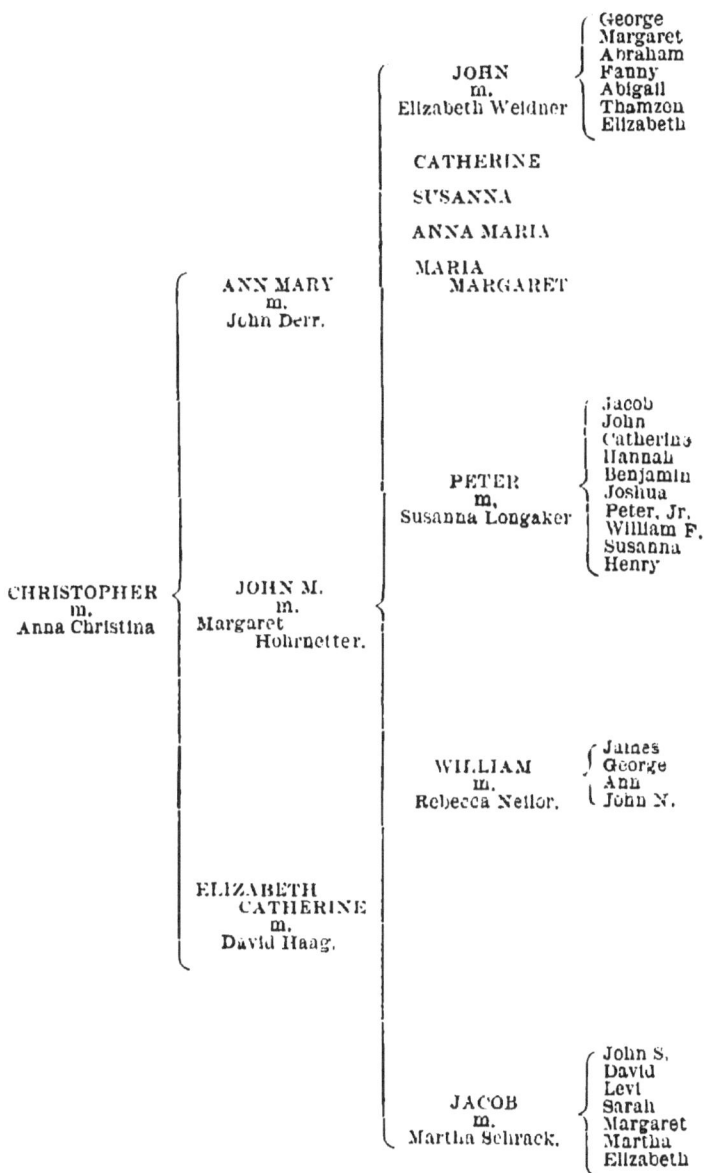

CHRISTOPHER
m.
Anna Christina

- ANN MARY
  m.
  John Derr.

  - JOHN
    m.
    Elizabeth Weidner
    - George
    - Margaret
    - Abraham
    - Fanny
    - Abigail
    - Thomzon
    - Elizabeth
  - CATHERINE
  - SUSANNA
  - ANNA MARIA
  - MARIA
  - MARGARET

- JOHN M.
  m.
  Margaret Hohrnetter.

  - PETER
    m.
    Susanna Longaker
    - Jacob
    - John
    - Catherine
    - Hannah
    - Benjamin
    - Joshua
    - Peter, Jr.
    - William F.
    - Susanna
    - Henry
  - WILLIAM
    m.
    Rebecca Neilor.
    - James
    - George
    - Ann
    - John N.

- ELIZABETH
- CATHERINE
  m.
  David Haag.

- JACOB
  m.
  Martha Schrack.
  - John S.
  - David
  - Levi
  - Sarah
  - Margaret
  - Martha
  - Elizabeth

Index to Illustrations.

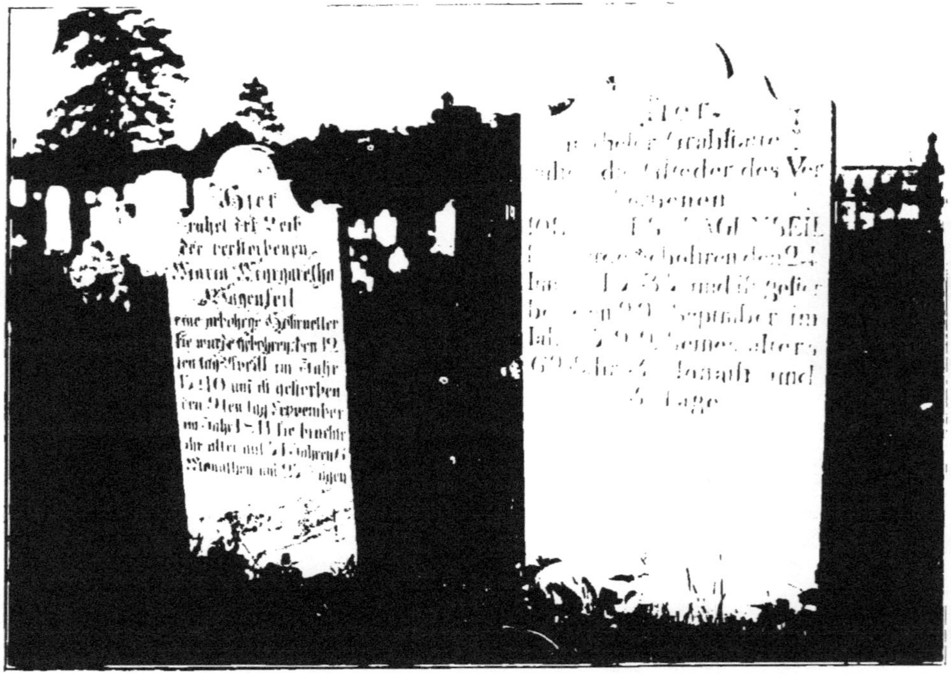
Hier
ruhet der Leib
der verstorbenen
Wagenseil

History of Wagenseller Family.

1. CHRISTOPHER¹ WAGENSEIL.—The first evidence discovered of the name "Wagenseller" in this country was prior to 1734. It was then spelled "Wagenseil". In "Rupp's Collection of Thirty Thousand Immigrants" who arrived at the port of Philadelphia between 1727 and 1776, the name does not appear. On page 474, however, of the same volume under the heading, "Names of 465 German, Dutch and French Inhabitants residing in Philadelphia County prior to 1734," there is found the name of "Stoffel Wagenseil" who paid a quit rent on 150 acres of land in Hanover township.

At that time and up to 1784, what is now Montgomery County was included in Philadelphia County, Pa. In 1734 Hanover township comprised all of the present townships of New Hanover, Upper Hanover, Douglass and Pottsgrove and the borough of Pottstown. In 1741 it was divided into the first three townships named. The quit rent mentioned above is a reserved rent in the grant of land, by the proprietary by the payment of which the landholder was to be freed from the other taxes. Quit rents were not uniform; they varied from one shilling sterling per hundred acres to six shillings per annum and in other instances more.

Hanover township, as it existed in 1734, covered the whole northern part of what is now Montgomery County. It lies in the Valley of the Perkiomen creek. That entire region, in the pioneer days, was called *Falck-ner Schwamm*—in English Falkner Swamp), after Daniel Falkner the agent of the Frankfort Company. On the 25th day of October 1701, William Penn issued letters Patent granting to the Frankfort Company composed of inhabitants of the city of Frankfort-on-the main, in Germany, and represented in Pennsylvania by their attorneys, Daniel Falkner and Johannes Jawert, a tract of land * * * known as the great tract containing 22,377 acres. It comprised pretty nearly what was Hanover township in 1734, when we have the first record of Stoffel Wagenseil. Stoffel is a nickname or German name for Christopher and Rupp's way of spelling "Wagenseiler" is probably an error as the name in that day was spelled Wagenseil—a purely German name.

What part of Europe Christopher Wagenseil came from has not been fully established. There are hosts of the pioneers from that section who came from Palatinate in Germany. Frequently a shipload of people coming from the same locality in Germany would settle in the same locality in the new world, but this does not by any means prove that Christopher came from Germany. There are among the older generation of the descendants living, who think they have had traditional information that the founder of the Wagenseller family upon this continent came originally from Holland. This question remains to be determined positively as well as the time he arrived at the port of Philadelphia. There are no complete lists of arrivals prior to 1717 and the writer is not sure there were any at all. In 1717, the Provincial Governor Keith and his cabinet became alarmed at the great influx of foreigners and ordered lists of all immigrants deposited with the government. It was also ordered that all foreigners must take the oath of allegiance to the Crown. Christopher may have come over prior to 1717 or between 1717 and 1727. Then again the lists are not complete. Quite often there was sickness upon the arrival of the vessel and the sick were isolated and became absorbed with the people of the frontier without taking the oath of allegiance. This probably explains why there is no record of our ancestor's arrival.

The name of his wife as given in his will on file in City Hall, Philadelphia, is Anna Christina. They were, no doubt, married before coming to this country, as upon the church records of that region, which then were well kept, we find no record of ther marriage.

Christopher evidently did not retain his original possession of 150 acres of land or else he sold off a portion of it to some one else. Nearly all the early settlers in this region secured their land from the Frankfort Company through their American agent, Daniel Falkner, but we have no record of Christopher having secured his from them, but it is probable that he did as the Frankfort Company had possession of the entire Perkiomen region. It seems from his will that the tract Christopher owned prior to his death contained only 101 acres and this was again reduced to 50 acres by a sale to his son in-law, David Haag. Whether this was a part of this original 150 acres we have not been able to determine. We append a copy of the will which explains itself. Upper Hanover township is in the extreme north-eastern corner of Montgomery County, in the vicinity of Pennsburg. As taken from the records the Will is as follows:

WILL No. 222, AT CITY HALL, PHILADELPHIA, PA.

BOOK M., PAGE 387.

MADE JUNE 13, 1760, PROBATED OCT. 22, 1762.

WAGENSEIL, CHRISTOPHER.

In the name of God, Amen, whereas, I Christopher Wagenseil, of Upper Hanover township, in the county of Philadelphia and province of Pennsylvania, yeoman, find myself in an advanced age and very weak in body but of sound mind and memory, thanks be to God, therefore call-

ing to mind the mortality of my body and knowing that
it is appointed for all men once to die, therefore do I make,
publish and declare this my last will and testament in the
following manner, that is to say, *Imprimis*, I give and
bequeath to my only son, John Wagenseil, my plantation
situate in Upper Hanover township in the county of
Philadelphia aforesaid adjoining the land of Jacob Hystaad
and Jacob Moyre containing about 50 acres of land, be
the same more or less, it being part of one hundred and
one acres of land, the remainder having been formerly
sold and released by me to my son-in-law, David Haag,
with the condition that the Perkiomen creek shall be the
division line between the said 2 tracts, together with the
house, outhouses, barn, stables and all that is nailfast to
the buildings, with all the cleared land, meadows, orchards,
garden fencing and whatever is improved thereon so as it
at present doth stand.   Together also with one horse, one
mare and a colt of 2 years old and three cows, one heifer,
one calf, six sheep and four lambs and two hogs as also
one cart, the plow and swingle tree and what belongs to it
together with the collars and gears, the saddle, and bridles,
the table, the iron stove, the iron kettle, the largest iron
pot, one chest, the gun, two axes, croping hoe, a mall and
two wedges, a hatchet, dung hook and forks, together with
all sorts of household goods and tools together also with
eight shears with winter corn in the ground.   To have
and hold my said plantation and tract of land with the improvements with all and every other the appurtenances
aforesaid unto my said son, John Wagenseil, and to his
heirs and assigns and to their only only proper use and
behoof forever.   But all that subject, under and with the
following conditions and restrictions, that is to say, that I
hereby accept and reserve for myself and my wife, Anna
Christina, full privilege and liberty to live upon the said
plantation in the house where we now live until the time
of our death and my said son John shall yearly give to us
during our life time nineteen bushels of Rai and five bushels of wheat, two bushels of buckwheat, one bushel of
Indian corn and one fat hog to weigh one hundred and

fifty pounds weight and shall keep and hold for us a cow in his fodder in summer and winter time as good as his own, for our use and shall yearly plough and sow for us one-quarter acre with flax seed, he shall also yearly give us six pounds of wool. I except and reserve also for myself and my wife the half part of the small kitchen garden and part of the other cabbage land and garden and also the equal third part of the apples, peaches and whatever grows in the orchard. They shall also have liberty to take as much turnips as they may have necessary for their own use. He, the said John Wagenseil, shall give to his said father and mother the sum of thirty-five shillings, lawful money of Pennsylvania and shall cut yearly fire-wood for them as much as they may have necessary during their lifetime and further do I give and bequeath to my eldest daughter, Anna Mary, now the wife of John Dur [Dirr] the sum of 25 pounds. lawful money of Pennsylvania, and to her heirs and assigns to be paid her by my said son, John Wagenseil, or his heirs, or successors, one year after the death of me and my wife, Christina, and further do I give and bequeath to my youngest daughter, Elizabeth Catherine, now the wife of David Haag and to her heirs and assigns the sum of 25 pounds, lawful money of Pennsylvania to be paid her by my said son, John Wagenseil, or his heirs or successors two years after the death of me and my wife as aforesaid, and I do hereby further, with the consent of my wife, Anna Christina, give and beq'th to my said two daghts my beding and chest with the clothing belonging to my said wife that the same may be equally divided among and between them, after the death of my wife with the condition that all my remaining household goods and tools shall be and remain for my said son, John Wagenseil, and for his heirs and assigns or ever as above mentioned and further it is my will that in case any more money shall be required for the payment of my land then agreed on with my son-in-law, David Haag that the same shall also be paid by my son, John W. or his heirs or successors, and I do hereby desire,

that all may be done and performed according to this my
last will and testament but further is it my will that as
concerning our yearly subsistence that after the death of
the one or of the other of us the half of the abovesaid particulars shall cease and determine and only the half part
thereof be given by my said son to that, that may survive
the other, and I do hereby certify, nominate and appoint
my beloved wife, Anna Christina, to be the sole executrix of
this my last will and testament and I do hereby declare this
and no other to be my last will and testament in witness
and confirmation whereof I have to this my last will and
testament set my hand and seal on this thirteenth day of
June Anno Domini, one thousand seven hundred and sixty.

[Signed] Christopher Wagenseil.

Signed, sealed, published and declared by the said
Chris. Wagenseil as and for his last will and testament.
In the presence of us as witnesses:

JOHN MARTIN,
FREDERICK LIMBACH,
DAVID SHULTZ.

Phila., Pa., 27 October 1762, there personally appeared Frederick Limbach and David Shultz, two of the
witnesses to the foregoing will and thes. Frederick
Limbach on oath and thes. David Shultz on his solemn
affirmation according to law did declare he saw and hear-
ed Chris. W.————the testator therein named, sign, seal,
publish and declare the same for and as his last will and
testament and that at the doing thereof he was of sound
mind, memory and understanding to the best of their
knowledge. WILLIAM RUMSTED, Reg. Gen'l.

Be it remembered that on 27 October 1762, the last
will and testament of Chris. W.————,dec'd, in due form
of law was proved and probated and letters testamentary
were granted to Anna Christina W., executrix, in the said
deceased estate and to bring an inventory thereof into the
Regd. Gen. office at Phila. on or before the 27 of Nov.
next and render a true account when thereunto legally re-

quired. Given under the seal of the said office.

WM. RUMSTED, Regd. Gen'l.

The above document itself discloses considerable information concerning Christopher, who is the ancestor of a great many hundred descendants, both living and dead. From this we learn that Christopher and Anna Christina had three children

+ 2.   i.   ANN MARY².

+ 3.   ii.   ELIZABETH CATHERINE.

+ 4.   iii.   JOHN.

2. ANN MARY,² (*Christopher*¹).—Of the daughters of Christopher Wagenseil, very little has been discovered at this late date. Ann Mary married John Derr. It is said that John Derr at one time owned the land where the town of Pennsburg now stands. The records of the old Lutheran church at Pennsburg were gone over by Rev. O. F. Waage, the present pastor, who has not been able to find any record concerning the birth or marriage of these people. There was found, however, a record of baptism as follows :

Elizabeth Catherine, daughter of John and Anna Maria Derr, born Nov. 11, 1760, baptized Nov. 14, 1760. Sponsors, David and Elizabeth Haag.

In Henry S. Dotterer's "Pennsburg Region," page 39, from the docket of Michael Croll, Justice of the Peace, is taken:

"June 4, 1787, John Derr assigned John Lesh to Jacob Zepp to serve him the remainder term of his indenture."

There was a Lorentz Derr living in that region at the same period who was probably a brother of John. We find a record, "Sarah, daughter of Lorentz and Maria Derr, born May 28, 1762, baptized May 30, 1762," and "John Martin, son of Lorentz and Maria Derr, born Feb. 18, 1760. Sponsors, Martin and Maria Gertrude Derr." The name Derr is still prominent in Montgomery County. Franklin Derr, a marble cutter from the upper end of Montgomery County, went to Norristown prior to 1850 and amassed a fortune. One of the monuments of his skill is the Montgomery County Court House, at Norristown, Pa. One of his sons is still living there. Samuel S. Derr resides in Pottsgrove township.

3. ELIZABETH CATHERINE² (Christopher¹).— She was married to David Haag some time between 1748 and 1758 as taken from the records of the Goshenhoppen church. David and George Haag arrived from Europe Sept. 7, 1748. David's age is given as 22, hence born 1726, probably in Germany. During the latter part of the last century the name Haag seems to have been all through that section of the state, all perhaps descendants of David and George. This name like that of Wagenseller has entirely disappeared from the assessment lists of Montgomery County. It may have changed to Haak or Hawk, names that are now scattered through that section. In Rev. Casper Stoever's record, 1730-1779, the name appears frequently. In this list we find that Elizabeth [Wagenseller] Haag was a sponsor at the baptism of John George Haag, born July 9, 1758, baptized July 23, 1758, a son of George Haag, Jr., and wife Anna Margar of Northkill.

4. JOHN² (Christopher¹).—According to Christopher's will previously given, this is his only son, without whom the name Wagenseller would not now be in America and from whom all bearing the name are descendants. There seems to be discrepancy in the records of his birth. From the old Pennsburg church records we glean:

"John, son of Christopher and Christina Wagensell, born June 24, 1739, baptized July 15, 1739. Sponsors, John and Anne Maria Bast." On his tombstone in the old church at the Trappe it says, he was born June 24, 1737 which corresponds to his age on the tombstone. The former is probably correct as the error was more likely to occur through the lapse of time. He was confirmed in the Lutheran church near Pennsburg, Philadelphia County, Pa., at the age of 14 years on Good Friday 1853. This too would seem to prove that he was born in 1739. He married Margaret Honnetter, a native of Montgomery County and a daughter of Andrew Honnetter, who owned a farm in Douglass township, by deed dated Jan. 1, 1750, of 107 acres and 100 perches. The will of Andrew Honnetter is dated April 2, 1777, and John Wagenseller and Barned Gilbert are the executors. In the records of the New Hanover Church, located 6 or 7 miles west of Pennsburg and 5 miles north-east of Pottstown, we find the baptismal record of Andrew, son of Andrew and Dorothy Honnetter, born May 2, baptized June 25, 1758. The son, Andrew, is a brother of John Wagenseller's wife and the others are her parents. The graves of her parents are in the New Hanover Church yard within 3 yards of the present building. The original New Hanover Church was erected in 1767 and the present church is the third edifice. The Honnetter graves are marked:

Andrew's is a red Triassic sandstone with a German inscription partly illegible. Translated it reads: "Here rests the body of Andrew Honnetter * * * * Dec. 19, 1711 and died Apr. 26, 1777." This is only 3½ weeks after he made his will, above mentioned. The other, a blue Norristown marble with the German inscription well preserved: Here rests one who died a member of this church, Dorothy Honnetter. She was born October 28, 1717, and died March 14, 1792, aged 74 years, 6 months and 15 days. She was the wife of Andrew, born 1711. In volume XVII, Pa. Archives, 2nd series, p. 177, "Johannes Honetter arrived Oct· 30, 1738, aged 36," hence born 1702 and Andrew was born 1711. They were doubtless brothers and Andrew, for some reason, failed to qualify. Such cases are not infrequent. Quite a number of the passengers of the vessel in which Johannes arrived settled at New Hanover. This has been corrobated. Another person of the same name is found though differently spelled. Anna Barbara Hornecker (1737–1812) married George Peter Hillegas (1637–1810). They were the ancestors of Rev. Michael Reed Minnich, the well-known historian and author, who now resides at 3200 Powelton

Ave., Philadelphia. Valentine Honnetter, born Dec. 8, 1778, was in Captain Philip Hahn's Company, Fourth Battalion, Regiment of foot, commanded by Colonel Wm. Dean, in the army of the Revolution.

Andrew Honnetter married Margaret Gotshall Mar. 28, 1750.

Catherine Honnetter married Henry Schweinhard Jan. 22, 1799. These two marriages are taken from the record in the New Hanover Church. What relation Anna Barbara, Andrew and Catharine have to our ancestor, the wife of John Wagenseller, we have not discovered, but we give the data here for the benefit of those who wish to make an additional research. John Wagenseller and his wife, Anna Margaret, were the sponsors for Anna Margaret, daughter of Henry Engel and wife, Catherine, daughter born Oct. 25, 1763, baptized Feb. 26, 1764. It will be noted that here John Wagenseller's wife's name is given as Anna Margaret and on the tombstone it is Mary Margaret. Henry Engel and wife, in turn, were the sponsors for Catherine, born Dec. 3, 1764, baptized Apr. 7, 1765, a daughter of John and Margaret Wagenseller, an account of whom will be given in regular order in this work. If Engel's were not related, they must have been near neighbors.

We now come to the details of the life of John, the only male representative of the Wagenseller family in this country. Like his father, he followed the occupation of a farmer. Having inherited the 50 acres on the Perkiomen from his father, he tilled this soil for some time, but we we have no means of knowing how long. His father died in 1762 and then he certainly lived on the Perkiomen, and even in 1754 when his daughter, Catherine, was baptized by the pastor of the New Hanover Lutheran Church, we might suppose he still lived there, but this is no proof as in those times the pastor of the N. H. L. church was also pastor of the Lutheran church at Trappe or New Providence in Providence township, now divided into Upper Providence and Lower Providence. At any rate John and his family moved to Providence township near the old Trappe church. There he died as did also his wife. Both are buried in the old grave yard. B. F. Schlicher, who for eleven years was sexton of the church and cemetery, writes concerning their graves: "They have tombstones planted in the ground. The graves are not in a very nice condition." Dr. B. F. Wagenseller of Selinsgrove visited the cemetery some years ago and corroborates the statement of the sexton. The inscriptions are:

> Johannes Wagenseil,
> born June 24, 1737,
> died Sept. 29, 1799,
> aged 62 years, 3 mos. and 5 days.

> Mearia Meargartha Wagenseil, a born Hohrnetter,
> born April 12, 1740,
> died Nov. 9, 1811,
> aged 71 years, 6 mo., 27 days.

The papers relative to the settlement of John Wagenseller's estate are on file in the court house at Norristown. In these papers some peculiar ways of spelling the names are observed. In most places it is spelled Waggonseller and in a deed given by John's heirs written by his son, Peter, the name is spelled Waggonsailer. It appears that John stuck to the original German name as it is found upon his tombstone and his children after numerous experiments finally adopted the present form, Wagenseller, which is used by all the descendants except the descendants of Amos and Thomas Weidner, sons of George Wagenseller of the Wabash, a grand son of the one now under consideration. They spell it Wagonseller. The inventory is as follows:

AN INVENTORY

of the goods and chattels of John Waggonseller, deceased, taken this 14th day of October 1799 by the subscribers. Sworn August 14th 1799. Appraisers { Henry Pawling.
Wm. R. Atlee, Register. { John Shannon.

	£.	s.	d.
To wearing apparel,	8	15	
To horse saddle and bridle,	25	10	
To cash in the house,	9	3	2
To bonds in the house,	572	10	
To book accounts,	308	19	10
To ten plate stove,	6		
To one ditto,	5		
To one breakfast table,	1	10	
To 1 dining table,	1	2	6
To 2 ditto,		12	6
To 1 clothes press,	8		
To 24 hour clock,	5		
To cupboard,	1	10	
To a case of drawers,	2		
To books,	1		
To Philis' time,	7	10	
To 1 old stove,		7	6
To old lady's bed, bedstead and curtains,	7	10	
To 13 table cloths,	2		
To 2 bed cases,		15	
To 5½ yds. check,		16	6
To 8 sheets, 1 bed cover and 2 pillow cases,	2	8	
To 1 coverlid,	2		
To 1 table cover,		5	
To 2 yds. calimanes,		6	
To scatacklings in bofet,	1		
To 14 chairs,	2	10	
To 2 pair of cards,		5	
To 1 pair sheep shears,		1	6
To 1 gun,		15	
To a small looking glass,		2	
To a new spinning wheel,	1		
To 2 old ditto,		10	
To upper feather bed,		15	
To 1 bed and bedstead,	2		
To 1 ditto,	1	17	6
To 1 chaff bed,	2	10	
To 1 old ditto,	2	10	

	£.	s.	d.
To yarn for a coverlid,		17	6
To 12 lbs. woolen yarn,	2		
To 4¾ ton yarn,		5	
To 1 old chest with drawers,		3	9
To 1 pillow and some cotton,	1		
To 2 hemp hackels,	1		
To 1 looking glass,		7	6
To bed and bedstead,	2		
To 1 chest with drawers,		10	
To ½ share of hoop net,		5	
To 14 lbs. sole leather,	1		
To 1 old cart and some flax seed,	1		
To a bed and bed stead,	3		
To a lot of upper harness leather,		10	
To 21 bee hives and straw stand,	1	5	
To 1 pair butter boxes and sundries,	1	7	6
To 1 cask vinegar, some salt and old casks,		15	
To 4 lbs. feathers and wagon cover,	1	10	
To 2 looms and lot of gears,	7	10	
To 4½ lbs. wooling yarn,		13	6
To 1 dresser with a platte on it,	3	10	
To 1 pair stillards,		7	6
To 1 doughtrough,		2	6
To 1 clover seive,		7	6
To 30 earthen pots,		6	
To 6 cedar buckets,		6	
To 3 cedar tubs,		15	
To churn and kealler,	6	5	
To 1 dripping pan and sundries,		5	
To 2 kettles, 1 gridiron, 1 bake oven and 1 frying pan,	1	4	
To 3 flatirons,		7	6
To 1 coffee mill, 3 candle sticks, 3 lamps and 1 box iron,		7	6
To 1 pair andirons, 2 pair of tongs, 1 shovel and pot rack,	1	10	
To 1 pair of bellows, camp kettle and candle moles,		6	6

	£.	s.	d.
To 1 watering pot, 1 earthen jug, weights and scales and 13 lbs. bees wax,	1	5	6
To 2 augers, 2 hand saws, whip saw and drawing knife,		10	6
To 4 weeding hoes, spade, 2 shovels and grubbing hoe,		10	
To large brass kettle, iron kettle, dutch oven,	4	5	
To iron bar pick, mall and wedges, 3 old axes,		15	9
To lot of old iron, 10 old sickles,	1	2	6
To 1 scythe and cradle, grindstone, 3 scythes and sneads,	1	9	9
To 3 hhds., 3 barrels and 6 old casks,	1	10	6
To 1 wheelbarrow, 1 sled and 1 stage wagon,	7	17	
To 1 apple mill,	2	10	
To 16 bags, 8 bushels buckwheat, 13 bu. rye,	6	9	
To 1 windmill, half bushel, etc.,	2	6	9
To 8 rakes, 2 pitchforks, cutting box,	1	9	
To 2 turnip knives, 1 old saddle and bridle,		12	
To 4 chains, 1 hobble, 2 dung forks,		16	3
To 1 dung hook, 2 plows, 2 harrows, wagon, slay,	18	17	6
To 14 hives of bees, 2 single trees, 4 chairs,	7	11	6
To 3 set of horse gears and collars, 2 pair rope traces, 2 cruppers,	3	9	
To 15 tons of hay, 500 sheaves of oats,	62	10	
To 40 bushels of rye, 70 bundles of flax,	9	10	
To 1 blind mare and 3 colts,	25	10	
To 1 beef cow,	3		
To 1 white cow,	4	10	
To 1 brindle cow,	4	10	
To 1 bell cow,	4	10	
To 1 black cow,	2	10	
To 1 young cow,	3		
To 2 bulls and 1 heifer,	6		
To 12 sheep,	4	10	
To 11 acres of Indian corn in the ground,	22	10	
To a lot of corn fodder,	1	10	

	£.	s.	d.
To 11 acres of wheat and rye in the ground,	22		
To 7½ acres of land,	15		
To a patch ot potatoes and pumpkins,		15	
To 2 large hogs,	6		
To 2 large hogs,	5		
To 6 shoats,	5		
To 25 bushels of buckwheat at Longacre's,	2	6	10
To 2 shoats,		17	6
To some buckwheat on the premises computed, to be 25 bushels,	2	10	
To ½ of the seine and boat,	2		
To 1 wool wheel,		16	

£1306 1 4

ESTATE ACCOUNT.
[dated Nov. 7, 1801.]

The account of John and Peter Wagenseller, administrators of the estate of John Wagenseller, late ot Providence township, Montgomery County, deceased.

The accountant charges themselves.   Dr.

	£.	s.	d.
To amount of inventory filed in the Register's office at Norristown,	1310	2	2
To advance in sale of goods,	109	11	10

£1419 s14

Errors excepted.
                John Wagenseller,
                Peter Wagenseller,
Affirmed and subscribed, 7 Nov. 1801.
                        THOMAS POTTS, Regst.
Pd. Contra the pray allowance.

	£.	s.	d.
By cash paid register for letters of administration,	1	4	8½
By cash paid for stamped paper,		4	2½

	£.	s.	d.
By cash paid for proving appraisements and expenses, etc.,	1	18	5
By cash paid John Pawling,		7	8
By " " John Adams,	3		
By " " Crawford & Long,	2	4	6
By " " John Essick,	1	17	6
By " " David Sower,		7	6
By " " William Gray,		7	6
By " " Isaac Jacobs,	3		
By " " Thomas Mason,	1	19	4½
By " " Moses Jones,		16	6
By " " Jacob Longanacre,	1		2
By " " Derrick Casseberry,		15	10
By " " Peter Wagenseller, two notes and interest,	12	12	
By cash paid Morris Jones,		4	4½
By " " Lewis Horning,	7		
By " " John Riner,	1	18	6
By " " Jacob Clinger,	14	14	2
By " " David Sower,		7	6
By " " Dr. Isaac Huddleson,		18	9
By " " Philip Hummelright,	55	15	
By " " Peter Madders Vendue Cryer,	5	12	6
By " " Samuel Keen Poor Tax,	1	9	3
By " " Conrad Swineford,	2	9	
By " " Robert Tyson,		10	2
By " " John McCleland,	1	17	6
By " " John Edwards,		15	
By " " Nathan Potts for I. Markley,	1	2	9
By " " Robert Miller,	1	19	1
By " " Thomas Adams,		17	9
By " " David Widener,	5	18	10
By " " Benjamin Royer,	2	11	
By work done by Peter and William on the plantation after the decease of their father about 1 month and a quarter each,		7	10
By William Wagenseller threshing the grain,	3		

	£.	s.	d
By vendue expenses to Peter and William Wagenseller,	4	10	
By cash paid Elisha Evans Bond,	106		
By " " " " "	112		
By " " " " "	50	8	9
By commissisons on settling the above estate 4 per cent	56	15	8
By cash paid Register for filing amount, etc.,	1	16	3
By " " for presenting to court and certified copy,	1	2	6
By cash paid Clerk of Orphans' Court,		15	
By " " one year's interest on bond due Elisha Evans, due April 1, 1802,	6		
Balance due the estate,	938	11	5½
	£1419	14	0½

Montgomery County ss.

I, Thomas Potts, Esquire, Register for the probating of Wills and the granting of Letters of administration in and for the county of Montgomery, certify that a notice of the filing of the account of the estate of John Wagenseller, deceased, by the administrators was put up in my office and that due proof was this day made before me that three other notices were put up, one at Morris Jones', one at Valentine Shalor's and one at William Fitzgerald's—three of the most public places in the neighborhood of the parties—and that all the said notices were set up thirty days before the time agreeably to the Act of Assembly in such cases made and provided.

In witness whereof I have hereunto set my hand this ninth day of November one thousand eight hundred and one. GEO. M. POTTS, Dep'ty Regs't.

Montgomery County, ss.

Seal
of
County

I certify that at an Orphans' Court held at Norristown in and for the county of Montgomery held the tenth day of November in the year of our Lord one thousand eight hundred and

one before the Honorable John D. Coke, Esq., and his associate justices of the said court the within account was duly confirmed. Witness my hand and the seal of the said county.   T. Swaine.
True copy.

The signatures of John and Peter Wagenseller, administrators, are clear hair lines, regular and neat and evidently written with a good quill pen. The bond is dated October 14, 1799 to which their signatures are also attached. The children of John and Margaret Wagenseller, as recited in a deed on record at Norristown, are: John, Catherine married to Conrad King, Susanna married to Conrad Swinehart, Mary married to Benjamin Royer, Margaret married to Mathias Walter, Peter, William and Jacob. There were eight children the dates of whose births range as follows:

+   5.   i.   John, born Dec. 14, 1763.
+   6.   ii. Catherine, born Dec. 3, 1764.
+   7.   iii. Susanna, born Feb. 2, 1768.
+   8.   iv. Anna Maria, born May 20, 1770.
+   9.   v.   Maria Magaretha, born June 2, 1772.
+   10. vi. Peter, born Sept. 24, 1774.
+   11. vii. William, born May 25, 1778.
+   12. viii. Jacob, born   1782.

The above named children down to and including Anna Maria were baptized and are recorded on the books of the old Pennsburg church except Catherine. The records of the others are not found there. From the Trappe church records in the Pennsylvania German Society publications, we note that Maria Margaretha Wagenseil, born June 2, 1772, was baptized Nov. 1, 1772, hence John must have moved from Upper Hanover township to Providence township 1771 or 1772. In the assessment books of Providence township for 1785, John was assessed wite 125 acres, 4 horses and 4 cows; 1786, 125 acres, 3 horses and 4 cows. Amount of tax $5.50. His assessment continues down to 1799, the year of his death. Prior to 1784, the records were kept at Philadelphia and the assessment books for that period could not be obtained at the City Hall. The assessment of the 125 acres of land continues up to the time of his death. In addition to the land in 1798 John was assessed with 3 horses and 4 cows valued (including land) $1520, amount of tax $5.74. In 1799, 2 horses and 4 cows valued (including land) $1410, amount of tax $5.50. 1800, no assessment, he having died in 1799.

CHILDREN OF JOHN AND MARGARET WAGENSELLER.

We now take up the children of John and Margaret Honnetter Wagenseller and treat the record of each separately and in the order of their birth giving to each the consecutive number previously assigned.

5. JOHN³ (*John²*, *Christopher¹*) born Dec. 14, 1763, baptized Jan. 23, 1764. Sponsors, John and Magdalena Derr. He married Elizabeth Weidner Feb. 5, 1787. She is the daughter of Abraham and Margaret Weidner, born Sept. 25, 1767. The Weidner record is taken from an old family New Testament printed in German at Germantown, Pa., in the year 1769. John was the proprietor of the Red Lion Hotel in Uwchlan township, Chester County, Pa. He died August 5, 1811, at Red Lion Hotel, aged 47 years, 5 months and 21 days. His wife, Elizabeth, died Feb. 6, 1838, aged 71 years, 6 months and 11 days. Both lie buried in Pikeland cemetery, about 2 miles east of Chester Springs, Chester county, Pa.

They had seven children:

+ 13. i. George, born Jan. 8, 1788.
+ 14. ii. Margaret, born May 15, 1789.
+ 15. iii. Abraham, " Aug. 16, 1791.
+ 16. iv. Fanny, " July 10, 1793.
+ 17. v. Abagail, " May 17, 1795.
+ 18. vi. Thamsen, " June 18, 1797.
+ 79. vii. Elizabeth, " Sept. 14, 1800.

6. CATHERINE³ (*John²*, *Chistopher¹*), born Dec.

3, 1764, married Conrad King. They had nine children who will receive consideration elsewhere outside of the family tree. Catherine died 1820 at the age of 56 years and Conrad died in 1880 at the age of 80 years.

7. SUSANNA³, (John², Christopher¹), born Feb. 2, 1768, baptized Mar. 6, 1768. Sponsor, Susanna Honnetter. Married to Conrad Swinehart. We have very little information concerning the Swineharts. Some arrived from Europe Sept. 11, 1732 and others, Sept. 14, 1754. We have some Swinehart data which we will give for the benefit of those who wish to trace the connection. In the scope of our work we have not been able to do it.

Feb. 1, 1737, Joseph Mayhuw and Elizabeth Swinehart were married.

Mar. 3. 1795, Michael Sweinhart married Christina Gilbert.

1779.—Andrew Sweinhart signed a petition against calling a convention for the purpose of amending the constitution.

Married:

May 20, 1783, Schweinhard, Anna Maria to Michael Altendorfer.

Sept. 24, 1751, Schweinhard, Eva Barbara to Ludwig Pickel.

Dec. 9, 1746,   "   Eva Catherine to John Wm. Reifschneider.

Dec. 11, 1796, Schweinhard, Eva to Michael Reyer.

Oct. 20, 1805,   "   George to Susanna Sehler.

8. ANNA MARIA³, (John², Christopher¹), born May 20, 1770, Sponsors at baptism, John Derr and his daughter, Anna Maria. Married Benjamin Royer. He is probably a descendant of John Michael Reyer (Reier, Reiher, Royer) who is the founder of the family in Penn-·sylvania. He was born in Schwabbach, Wurtemburg, in the year 1686. His parents are John Michael and Anna Catherine Reiher. He married three times: First in the 170-, Anna Maria Seeland, daughter of Dietrick and

Amelia Maria Seland of Nuremburg. She died in 1742. Second, in the year 1743, Maria Catherine Schneider, daughter of Henrich Schneider and Catherina (maiden name Schuler) his wife of Aschpissen in the electorate of the Palatinate. Maria Catherina Schneider was born in 1713 and died in 1750. Third, Sept., 1751, Maria Christina Hœpler, a widow, born Nov. 18, 1718 in Borna, in the electorate of Saxony. John Michael Reyer with 2 sons came to America Sept. 1732. The former was the father of 24 children, ten with his first wife, six with the second and eight with the third and the husband of Anna Maria Wagenseller descends from this hardy stock.

9. MARIA MARGARET³, (*John²*, *Christopher¹*), born June 2, 1772, baptized Nov. 1, 1772. Sponsors, Peter Lange and Maria Margaretha. (Peter Lange arrived from Europe Sept. 15, 1749). She married Mathias Walter. From whom Mathias Walter descended we have no positive proof in our possession. The Pennsburg church records show that a Mathias Walter and a John George Walter, both old enough to be the father of Margaret's husband, lived in that section. It is probable that one of these was the ancestor of Margaret's husband. We append the data found on the records of the Pennsburg church for the benefit of those who desire to continue the search.

June 1, 1765, Mathias Walter was elected Elder.

John George, son of Mathias and Elizabeth Catherine Walter, born March 5, 1742, baptized June 4, 1742. Sponsors, George and Margaretha Heilig.

Maria Barbara, daughter of Mathias and Anna Maria Walter, born Feb. 1, 1757 and baptized Mar. 6, 1757.

Anna Margaretha, daughter of Mathias and Anna Maria Walter, born May 2, 1758, baptized May 14, 1758.

OTHER RECORDS, MISCELLANEOUS SOURCES.

Jacob Walter, Phila. County, took the oath of allegiance Sept. 7, 1740.

Mar. 28, 1750, Matthew Walter married Ann Maria Haag.

Apr. 25, 1817, Catherine Walter died, aged 56 years.

Aug. 18, 1787, Catherine Maria Walter died, aged 18 years.

Sept. 1, 1839, Margaret Walter died, aged 81 years, 10 months and 21 days.

July 13, 1846, George Walter died, aged 83 years, 9 months and 20 days.

The Walters in this country are very numerous. One Jacob Walter came from Europe about the middle of the last century and settled in Snyder County. From him descended hundreds most of whom are now living near the spot where Jacob originally settled about two miles from Middleburg, Pa. Many of Jacob's descendants have taken Horace Greely's advice and have gone west. It some one were to investigate, the result would be, the discovery of a connecting link that would prove all of these descendants from the same common source—including Margaret Wagenseller's husband.

10. PETER[8], (John[2], Christopher[1]), born in Montgomery (then Philadelphia) county, Pa., Sept. 24, 1774, was married in Lower Providence township, Montgomery county, to Susanna Longaker, Jan. 7, 1800, by Rev. Henry Geisenheimer. Susanna Longaker was born in Chester county, Pa., Jan. 28, 1781. The ancestry of Susanna is distinguished. In 1733, Ulrich Longenecker (Longaker) aged 69 years came from Europe. tradition says from Switzerland near Zurich and landed in Philadelphia Aug. 28, 1733 and took the oath of allegiance. He came in the ship Hope of London, Daniel Reed, master and with him were Ulrich, Jr., aged 22 years, and Jacob aged 19 years. It is probable that Ulrich, Jr. and Jacob were sons of Ulrich, Sr., at any rate, we have proof that Jacob, the 19 year old immigrant, is the grand father of Peter Wagenseller's wife. About 1746 Jacob Longenecker married Susanna Longenecker, the widow of John. (Probably Jacob's cousin.) Jacob and Susanna Longenecker had two sons, Jacob and Peter and five daughters, alome, wife of Jacob Bleim, Mary of Mr. Wisler, Esther

of Henry Rhodes, Magdalene of Jacob Ruth (now Root), Susanna of John Brower. Jacob, of the above list, married Catherine Detweiler, a daughter of John Detweiler. The family of John Detweiler consisted of four sons and nine daughters. Jacob Longaker (the name now changes) the father of Peter Wagenseller's wife was born Mar. 10, 1756 and died July 28, 1807, aged 51 yrs., 4 months and 18 days. Catherine, the wife of Jacob, was born Mar. 15, 1758, died March 10, 1816, aged 57 yrs., 11 mos. and 25 days. Susanna, the eldest daughter of this couple, is the person who became Peter Wagenseller's wife in 1800. She is said to have spoken German fluently, but that will not deny her Swiss ancestry. Her family in Switzerland has a coat of arms. Being questioned concerning her, his nephew, Hon. A. B. Longaker, of Norristown, writes :

Susanna Longaker Wagenseller, it is true, was the daughter of parents born in Chester County, whose language or speech in the family was German and German well spoken, and written by her ancestors. Her grandfather Jacob Langenecker, wrote his name to his will in good German penmanship. Daniel Langenecker, her uncle, I think a Mennonite preacher wrote a good German hand, both as regards orthography and penmanship. I have a photograph-ed letter under date of 1734, written by him. His son, David, was also a Mennonite preacher, and his signature is a fine specimen of German penmanship as appears by his will registered in Phila. The fact that this ancestry was educated Germans residing in Switzerland and by tradition of French origin, or as persecuted Huguenots de-parted from France about 1572. In civilization and by education many of these colonial settlers were at least 100 years educationally in advance of other Europeans.

"My father at the age of eight years did not speak the English language and removing into an English neighbor-hood when he was a young man, had lost all knowledge of speaking German and never again acquired it so that he could be said to be able to speak it well.

"Schools were established as early as 1750, both in Chester and Montgomery counties amongst the Longaker families, and Peter Longaker, my uncle, and amongst the eldest of the family was a school teacher. My uncle, Abraham, was a doctor. My father was a justice of the Peace, sheriff of the county, member of the House of Representatives two years, colonel of Militia and ten years one of the associate judges of the county. My aunt, Susan Longaker, was a lady of great information—full of knowledge of all the events of colonial times, of the family, etc., and a very pleasant and great talker, without a suspicion of German accent in her speech. It is probable she did not, like my father, forget her German speech, as she was amongst the oldest and my father of the youngest of the family."

Susannah died in Pekin, Tazewell County, Illinois, Apr. 29, 1862, aged 81 years, 3 months and 9 days.

Peter Wagenseller, having married only 7 days after the opening of this century, purchased a farm in Providence township and followed the occupation of a farmer. He must have attained some prominence as we learn from the history of Montgomery County p. 1056 that he was constable of Upper Providence township in 1809. On page 1048, we observe that he was elected jutice of the Peace, Dec. 4, 1816.

He was commissioned by the beloved Governor Simon Snyder, Dec. 24, 1816, and the same is recorded at Norristown. The following is a copy of the Commission:

SIMON SNYDER,

Seal of Com. of
Pennsylvania.   Pennsylvania ss.

In the name and by the authority of the Commonwealth of Pennsylvania, Simon Snyder, Governor of the said Commonwealth, to Peter Wagenseller of the county of Montgomery, Esquire, sends greetings: Know you that reposing especial trust, and confidence in your integrity, judgment and abilities, I, the said

Simon Snyder, have appointed and by these presents to appoint and commission you, the said Peter Wagenseller, to be a justice of the Peace in the district numbered two, composed of the townships of Providence, Limerick and Perkiomen in the county of Montgomery hereby giving and granting unto you full right and title to have and execute all and singular the powers, jurisdiction and authorities and to receive and enjoy all and singular the lawful emoluments of a justice of the Peace aforesaid agreeably to the constitution and laws of the Commonwealth. To have and to hold this commission and the office hereby granted unto you, the said Peter Wagenseller, as long as you behave yourself well. Given under my hand and seal of the state at Harrisburg this 24th day of December in the year of our Lord one thousand eight hundred and sixteen and of the said Commonwealth the forty-first.

By the Governor.   N. B. BOILEAN, Sec'y.
Recorded Feby. 3rd, 1817, at Norristown, in Book No. 2, page 11.

The old Peter Wagenseller homestead passed into the hands of the Pennypackers. Mr. John B. Pennypacker, born 1831, of Phoenixville, Pa,, writes: "The old house is just as it was sixty years ago, a very pretty old stone farm house. My father built the barn there and the long line of red cedars in front of the house and the white ash trees on the opposite side of the road I helped to plant. It is to-day quite a quaint and pretty home owned by a gentleman who, I think, resides in Philadelphia. I have traveled my share in our own country and from Portland to the Mississippi, I have never found a finer agricultural section than the surroundings of the home of your great grand-father, Peter Wagenseller. Susanna Wagenseller, old Peter's wife, was a sister of Judge Henry Longaker. His son, A. B. Longaker, of Norristown, was a member of the state legislature some years ago, and an ex-judge himself, Sept. 6, 1897." In 1887, Mr. Pennypacker wrote an article for the "Norristown Herald" which is so full of information that we will give it complete. It follows :

LETTERS FROM PORT PROVIDENCE.

THE FAMILIES AND FARMS OF SIXTY YEARS AGO— TIME'S CHANGES, &C.

Sixty years ago Peter Wagenseller owned the farm at present in possession of Thos. P. Walker, and lying one mile north of our village, having purchased it from John Jacobs, who was perhaps the largest land owner of this part of Gilbert's manor. The tract embraced about eighty acres. Old Peter had married Susan Longaker, a sister of the late Judge Henry Longaker, formerly of your bench, and his family consisted of six sons and two daughters, viz : Jacob, John, Benjamin, Joshua, Peter Jr., William, Catherine and Hannah. So that the old gentleman was pretty well fixed for help. Jacob, the eldest of the sons, studied medicine, and located at Selinsgrove, in Union County, where he married and soon built up for himself a fine reputation as a physician, and a lucrative practice. John, the second son, was a tailor by trade, and carried on his business in a little shop which stood a short distance south of the old house in which John Bartholomew, Sr., died, and near where his son, John, has, for the past forty odd years, carried on smithing; but he afterwards removed to the "Corner Stores" in Chester County. The little shop and the old house, like their tenants, have long since passed away.

Peter, Jr., died at the old home when about sixteen or seventeen years of age, and Benjamin, Joshua and William remained upon the farm with their father until some years later, when he sought a new home in the West. Of Peter's sons, John alone married here, marrying a Miss Norton, sister of Samuel Norton, who some thirty years ago resided in Phoenixville.

The daughters, Catherine and Hannah, married brothers, Matthew and Hamilton Chain, sons of old Matthew Chain, who formerly resided near Norristown. Old

Peter found his purchase to be a profitable one; prices of farm products were satisfactory, and his crops all he could. desire. So having accumulated some two or three thousand dollars in cash, he purchased the hills lying on the north side of Egypt road, which then, as at present, passed between the two tracts.

The price paid was seventy-five or eighty dollars per acre, without buildings of any kind whatever, which was certainly a pretty high figure.

The ensuing autumn the old man's corn cribs showed an exhibit of which any of our most practical farmers of to-day might feel a very just pride.

But prosperity often very unexpectedly takes wings, and this Mr. W. realized not many years later. When the upper or hill tract was purchased, a mortgage was given, which covered not only that, but also the first tract or purchase of 80 acres. A "tidal wave" of low prices set in, and eventually the entire tract fell back into the hands of the original owners—Penn's heirs—at the nominal price of $13 or $14 per acre. We think Gen. Cadwallader, of Philadelphia, afterward acted as agent of the Penns for this property, and it remained in his or their hands until about 1848 or '49, when it was purchased by Joseph S. Pennypacker of Gen. Cadwallader, for thirty-six or thirty-eight dollars per acre. The tract at that time comprised one hundred and ninety-eight acres, but has since been cut up and sold to other parties, while the original tract is the pleasant home of Thomas P. Walker.

After Peter Wagenseller left the property it soon became a splendid blackberry patch, for it was overgrown with briers and bushes; and when we were boys, say thirty five years ago, we never thought of going anywhere else than here to fill our baskets with the choicest berries.

After the property was sold the old man sought out a new Egypt in the wilds of the west, whither he went with his family. Benjamin, William—still single—accompanied him, and John closed up his business, and with his wife and two children the party was complete. While on their journey West, John's wife had been in delicate health, grew worse and died. Not very long after, Catherine, who had been left a widow, together with Hamilton and his wife, also took up the subsequent idea of old Horace and decided to "go West." William, the youngest of the boys, did not remain with the family very long after they had left for the new El Dorado, but came back to Selinsgrove and studied medicine with his brother Jacob.

Old Peter never returned to witness what time had done for the Valley of the Schuylkill, and particularly to Gilbert's Manor, for He who calls but once for all has long since summoned him to the happy hunting ground above.

Thus one at least of the first families of sixty years ago has passed from our midst, and we have no one left of the name of Wagenseller in our vicinity to-day.

FELIX, per
JOHN B. PENNYPACKER.

Port Providence, May 4th, 1877.

In the spring of 1834, Peter went to the West as above stated. It seems that Peter's son, John, had a small tract of land and this was sold before departing for the West. There is on record at Norristown a deed dated Dec. 15, 1832 entered on book 65, page 50 for 3 acres in Upper Providence township deeded by John Wagenseller and his wife Mary Ann to John H. Umstead, Witnesses to the deed, Peter Wagenseller and Anthony Vanderslice. Acknowledged before Peter Wagenseller, Justice of the Peace, Dec. 15, 1832. The trip to the West (Ohio) was not made as easily then as it is now. Peter and his family drove out requiring about 20 days to make the trip. May 24, 1834, Peter wrote a letter to his brother William giving a full description of the journey. William's daughter, Mrs. Margaret Young, near Pheonixville, Pa. still has the letter in her possession. It is dated at Columbus, Ohio. His life in Ohio was exceedingly short for he died in Franklin county, Ohio, June 14, 1835, aged 59 years, 8 months and 20 days. His widow later moved to Pekin with her son, Joshua, and there died at a good old age.

There were ten children born to Peter and Susan Wagenseller, as follows:

+ 20.   i. Jacob, born Jan. 2, 1801.
+ 21.   ii. John, born Dec. 17, 1802.
+ 22.   iii. Catherine, born Nov. 29, 1804.
+ 23.   iv. Hannah, born Apr. 25, 1807.
+ 24.   v. Benjamin, born Nov. 4, 1809.
+ 25.   vi. Joshua, born July 5, 1813.
  26.   vii. Peter, born July 6, 1815, died at the old home, Sept. 10, 1830.
+ 27.   viii. William Findlay, born Nov. 15, 1817.
  28.   ix. Susanna, born May, 20, 1820, died May 27, 1820, aged 7 days.
  29.   x. Henry, born April 18, 1826, died Apr. 24, 1826, aged 6 days.

11. WILLIAM³, (*John²*, *Christopher¹*), born May 25, 1778, married Rebecca Neilór, who died Oct. 20, 1844. He was a hotel keeper in West Pikeland township, Chester County, Pa., and died July 22, 1868. To them were born 5 children:

  30.   i. James, born Nov. 28, 1808, married Harriet Hartman of Pikeland, now deceased. They had no issue. Residence, Philadelphia. He died July 15, 1868.
+ 31.   ii. George, born Aug. 17, 1812.
  32.   iii. Ann, born Apr. 14, 1815, married Frederick Holman, died June 23, 1885 at Chester Springs, Chester Co., Pa. They had one child, Wm. Wagenseller Holman, born Dec. 1834, married Lydia Katherine Wagenseller, daughter of Dr. Jacob Wagenseller. Catherine is dead, buried at Se-

linsgrove. A son of Wm. and Catherine, H. C. Holman, resides at 2544 North Eleventh Street, Philadelphia.

+ 33. iv. John Neilor, born April 11, 1817.

34. v. Margaret Hornetter, born Oct. 28, 1818, married John Young of Chester Springs, Chester County, Pa., Oct. 7, 1845, the latter having died March 7, 1895. Mrs. Young is still living in Chester County, about six miles from Phoenixville, Pa. She is the oldest female descendant of the Wagenseller family living to-day and the last and only survivor of the fourth generation in this country. John and Margaret Young had seven children as follows:

(1) William H. Young, born Apr. 12, 1847, married Jan. 30, 1873, Abbie A. McWilliams, who died July 26, 1895. They had two children, Charles, born Jan. 13, 1876 and Homer, born Apr. 27, 1878, now at Gettysburg College. Wm. resides at Anselma, Chester Co., Pa. (2) John Shafer Young, Sept. 20, 1848, married Rebecca Moses, resides at Anselma, Pa. No issue. (3) Joseph A. Young born April 19, 1851, married May 29, 1879 to Kate Mellon of Phoenixville. In 1878 he formed a co-partnership with A. E. Eachus establishing the firm of Eachus and Young, who are now one of the oldest mercantile firms in Phoenixville, Pa. No issue (4) Geo. Wagenseller Young, born Aug. 24, 1852, married Annie Bourne, Sunbury, Pa. He is now in the mer-

cantile business in Newton, Kansas. This union was blessed with three children, S. Cameron, Charlotte Bourne and Edna. (5) Franklin Young, born Apr. 1st, 1854, died in infancy. (6) Ella R. Young, born Dec. 30, 1856, married Dec. 12, 1877 to Sylvester Pennypacker of Chester Springs, Pa. To them are born two children, Chester C., born Jan. 5, 1879, and John Young, born May 29, 1883. (7) Annie M. Young, born Jan. 9, 1863, married Jan. 9, 1884 to Henry C. Dewees, now reside at Anselma, Pa., with 3 children, Margaret Young, born Oct. 4, 1888, J. Hanse, born Sept. 19 1890 and Ida Elizabeth, born Nov. 17, 1896.

JACOB,⁸ (*John²*, *Christopher¹*), born——1782, married Martha Shrack. The Shracks are a decidedly numerous branch in this country, hence it is impossible to get the correct line of ancestry of Martha without special research upon this line. No less than 5 male persons with the name came to this country. Johannes Shreyck, (Lancaster county) took the oath of allegiance July 3, 1743. Some Shreyck's (Shrack) arrived Aug. 28, 1733, and in 1717 John Jacob Schrack with two sons, John Joseph and Philip came to America. The Shracks are numerous in Montgomery County to-day, in fact, all over the eastern and central portion of Pennsylvania, especially in Union County. This is to be expected where there were so many immigrants.

John Jacob Shrack who came from Germany in 1717 settled in Providence township west of Perkiomen creek. He brought with him his wife, Eva Rosina, and 4 children. He was a Lutheran and joined with others of the New Hanover, Providence and Philadelphia congregations in 1733, in commending persons sent to Europe to collect

money to build churches in Pennsylvania and in 1735—
'39 in urging the ecclesiastical authorities in Germany to
send a suitable preacher to serve these congregations.
Muhlenburg came in the fall of 1742 in response to these
petitions. Shrack died in the early part of the same year
at the age of 63 years.

Muhlenburg landed at Philadelphia on Thursday,
November 25, 1742. The following Sunday he preached
at New Hanover and on Monday the 29th, wrote in his
diary: "Three elders of the congregation accompanied me
nine miles down to New Providence for the purpose of
confering with the deacons here and stopped with the widow
Shrack, whose husband, a deacon, and one of those who
often petitioned the Rev. Mr. Ziegenhagen for a minister,
died the past summer." John Jacob Shrack was naturalized in the year 1729. He kept a public house, called the
Trap, which gave name to the village, which is retained
to the present day. His widow and afterward his sons,
continued the public house, which was widely known. In
the church register of the Lutheran church at the Trappe
is the Shrack family record, placed there probably by
Rev. John Casper Stoever, the predecessor of Muhlenburg.
From an old subscription list of the Trappe church dated
1760 for the support of Rev. Muhlenburg, pastor of New
Providence Lutheran Congregation, we find John Schrack
gave one pound, ten shillings, Jacob Schrack, 15 shillings
and Christian Schrack, 12 shillings. Only one other gave
as much as Jacob and no one gave more. The children
of John Jacob and Eva Rosina Schrack were;

Born in Germany.—John Joseph, born Oct. 9, 1712;
Naturalized in 1729 or 1730.

Philip, born Jan. 21, 1714, married Maria————.
They had issue: Jacob, born Nov. 29, 1740; John
born May 31, 1742; Henry, born Feb. 5, 1744;
Maria, baptized Apr. 17, 1748; Philip, born Nov. 3,
1750, baptized Apr. 1, 1751 (Rev. Henry Melchoir
Muhlenburg and his wife, Anna Maria, being the
sponsors). Maria, wife of Philip Schrack, was buri-

ed Sept. 23, 1766, aged 51 years.

Eva Barbara, born May 1, 1716, married John George Cressman, Dec. 9, 1735.

BORN AT SEA.—Maria, born at sea Oct. 26, 1717, married John Adam Simon Kun, Dec. 11, 1740. Her name is given in the record of marriage as Anna Maria Savina Schrack.

BORN IN PENNSYLVANIA.—John Jacob, born April 8, 1724, married Maria Elizabeth Muhlhahn, March 22, 1750.

Catherine, born July 17, 1726, married June 20, 1753 to Hugh Bradford, who was buried June 1, 1756 at the Trappe.

Christian, born Oct. 4, 1727.

Elizabeth, born April 13, 1729.

John Nicolaus, born June 23, 1730.

Widow Eva Rosina Schrack died October 19, 1756. She was a native of the imperial city of Ulm; married John Jacob Schrack in 1711. Her age was 68½ years. April 7, 1732, Jacob Schrack paid a quit rent of 18 shillings and 9 pence on 500 acres for 25 years in full (in Providence township.)

We have no data to prove that Martha Schrack is a descendant of John Jacob, but as Jacob Wagenseller lived in the very neighborhood with the Schracks, went to the same church with them, it was an easy matter for Jacob to meet Martha, gallant her to her father's home, whisper words of love and affection to her and invite her to join him in perpetuating the name Wagenseller for many a generation. This they did, for to them we credit a family of seven children:

+35.	i.	John Shrack, born Nov. 16, 1808.
+36.	ii.	David, born 1812.
+37.	iii.	Levi.
+38.	iv.	Sarah.
+39.	v.	Margaret.
+40.	vi.	Martha, born 1818.
+41.	vii.	Elizabeth, born Sept. 2, 1820.

13.   GEORGE⁴, (*John³, John², Christopher,¹*). Born
at Red Lion hotel, Chester county, Pennsylvania, January
18, 1788, married Leticia Cavender who was born October
3, 1788 and died September 29, 1863.   In 1821, we pre-
sume they lived in Beaver county, Pennsylvania, since
their son William says he was born there.   He moved to
Ohio in 1825.   In 1839 he moved to Crawford county,
Illinois.   Here George died April 18, 1857.   A letter
was published in the *Argus* printed at Robinson, the county seat of Crawford county, asking for information concerning some of George's descendants, but we failed to receive even a single reply.   Some of them as we shall see
later moved up to Terre Haute, Ind.   George lived near
the Wabash River and for want of a better distinction, we
have called him "George of the Wabash."

George and Leticia had seven children as follows:

+42.   i.   John Cavender, born July 24, 1813.
+43.   ii. Thomas Weidner, born Nov. 19,
                   1815.
+44.   iii. Abram, born Sept. 2, 1818.
+45.   iv. William, born June 24, 1821.
+46.   v.   Amos, born March 30, 1824.
47.   vi. Elizabeth, married Hugh Mathus
                   with whom she had three children,
                   Louisa born Oct. 21, 1848, died
                   1872. Martha born 1850, and
                   George born 1853.
48.   vii. Thamzen, born Oct. 15, 1830, and
                   died March 21, 1839.

14.   MARGARET⁴, (*John³, John², Christopher¹*), born
May 15, 1789, at the Red Lion hotel, married Benjamin
Ramsey and died Sept. 12, 1849 of Dropsy, aged 60 years,
3 month and 27 days.   Benjamin died Sept. 4, 1855, at
the age of 76 years.   He was a blacksmith and a wheel-
wright.   Both lie buried in the Goshen Baptist Church
burying ground, near West Chester, Chester county, Pa.
This union was blessed with a large family of twelve chil-

dren. (1) Joseph Wagenseller Ramsey, born Jan. 12, 1809, married March 11, 1841 to Albina Wollerton who died Jan. 30. 1878, aged 63 years. Joseph, her husband, died June 23, 1853 aged 44 years, 5 months and 11 days. Both are buried in the Goshen Baptist Church burying ground. They had three children. He was a school teacher. (2) Thomas Ramsey, born Sept. 10, 1812, married first, Ann S. Louden, died June 13, 1840, second, in 1850, Margaret E. Thomas. Thomas had one child with his first wife and three children with his second wife. He died Feb. 6, 1877 and is buried in the Goshen Baptist Church burying ground. (3.) Mary Ann Ramsey, born Aug. 28, 1815, died July 12, 1853, aged 37 years, 10 months and 15 days. Buried in Goshen burying ground with the others. She had one child. (4.) Sarah Ann Ramsey, born Feb. 8, 1818, married Feb. 27, 1860, to Joseph Lewis. She was the mother of two children and died Feb. 14, 1872. (5.) Elizabeth Ramsey, born Nov. 19, 1820, married William Walls and died Feb. 15, 1897 of pneumonia. She resided in Philadelphia, is the mother of one child and is now buried in the Goshen Baptist Church burying ground. (6.) Thamzen Ramsey, born March 3, 1823, married Dec. 11, 1843 to Juhh Hibberd, who died Aug. 16, 1862. Thamzen resided at West Chester, Pa., was the mother of two children and died of paralysis Sept. 28, 1897. (7.) Minerva Ramsey, born July 31, 1825, married Oct. 22, 1846, Richard Monroe Shepherd, who died Nov. 17, 1896. Minerva was the mother of six children and died Nov. 16, 1897. Mr. Shepherd and his wife formerly resided on their farm at the Grove, W. Whiteland township, Chester county, Pa. They were members of the Grove M. E. Church. Later they resided at Malvern, Chester county. Both are buried at Greenmount Cemetery, West Chester, Pa. (8.) John Weidner Ramsey, born Aug. 31, 1827. He went South and nothing has been heard of him since the war, when he was in Tennessee. (9.) Angeline Ramsey (Twin to Caroline), born March 7, 1830, married January 1, 1852 to Harry Ash who died Sept 10, 1896. She was the mother of seven children and died Jan. 31, 1892. Both are buried in Mt. Moriah Cemetery, Philadelphia, Pa. (10.) Caroline Ramsey, (Twin to Angeline), born March 7, 1830 and is now dead. No date given. (11.) Julia Ramsey, born Oct. 31, 1831, married first John Shepherd, now deceased, and second Isaac Massey, also deceased. She resided in Philadelphia, was the mother of three children with her first husband and one child with her second husband. She is buried in Greenmount Cemetery, West Chester, Pa., having died March 1, 1895. (12.) John Ramsey, born Nov. 4, 1810 and died Nov. 17, 1814.

15. ABRAHAM⁴, (*John³, John², Christopher¹*), born Aug. 16, 1791 at Lionville, Pa. Married Catherine Myers, daughter of Captain Thomas Henry Meyers of Philadelphia. He kept store at Red Lion, Pa. He died in Ottowa, Illinois, January 31, 1868. Catherine was born in 1800 and died June 28, 1847 at Glen Moore, Chester county, Pa. Their issue was 5 children:

+49.   i.   Julia Matilda,⁵ born Dec. 13, 1826.
+50.   ii.   Mary Elizabeth, born May 3, 1830.
+51.   iii. Thomas Meyers, born Aug. 14, 1833.
+52.   iv.   John Andrew, born Dec. 11, 1836.
+53.   v.   Emily Law, born Dec. 3, 1839.

16. FANNY⁴, (*John³, John², Christopher¹*), born July 10, 1793, married first ——— Evans, second Joseph Beidler, died Aug. 28, 1870. Buried in Green Mount in West Chester, Pa. She had one son with her first husband. All are dead.

17. ABIGAIL⁴, (*John³, John², Christopher¹*), born May 17, 1795, married Joseph John, near Yellow Springs, Pa., who was born July 11, 1790 and died April 15, 1833. Abigail died Feb. 17, 1855. Joseph and Abigail had six children as follows: (1.) Jerome John, born Dec. 28, 1815, died January 19, 1896, married Elizabeth J. Cornman, who died March 1895. Five children. (2.) Gates John, born Sept. 10, 1818, died July 19, 1896,

married Anna Maria Vandever. Widow resides in Phoenixville. Eleven children. (3.) Jeffery John, born March 6, 1823, died Nov. 22, 1883. Married Katherine Mason. Widow resides in Phoenixville, Pa. They had one son. (4.) Jason John, born May 2, 1825, died June 17, 1852, married Louisa Supples. They had one daughter. (5.) Park John, born April 17, 1828, never married, died Sept. 11, 1845. (6.) Joseph John, born Dec. 7, 1832, married Clemintina Green, now deceased. Joseph died Feb. 22, 1877. No issue.

18. THAMZEN⁴, (*John*³, *John*², *Christopher*¹), (Some places spelled Thamozin and Thamsen) born June 18, 1797, married John Marshall, son of Joseph Marshall of near Wilmington, Delware, May 22, 1816 at Philadelphia by William Staughton, D.D. Thamzen is buried in Green Mount in West Chester, Pa. Her husband went West and nothing was heard from him for years. He died out there. They had a family of six children. (1) Abraham Marshall, born March 17, 1819, died June 22, 1857. Wife died May 21, 1857, both are buried at Green Mount in West Chester. Three children are still living in New York. (1) Joseph Marshall, was born Aug. 17, 1821, he was married three times. With his first wife he had 6 children, with the second, 2 children. He resides at Batavia, Clearmont Co., Ohio. (3) Susan Crosley Marshall, born Sept. 14, 1823, married Henry Barrett Freeman, who died Feb. 12, 1878. Susan is still living in excellent health at the age of 75 years. They had six children. Three are living, one is W. H. M. Freeman, a successful jeweler at 18 and 20 Market Street, West Chester, Pa. (4) George Wagenseller Marshall, born Feb. 24, 1827, married first Amanda Ann Lewis, second Abigail Cecilia Jenkins, third Sarah Elizabeth Wilson. With the first wife, he had 2 children, second 4, third 3. Residence, 819 Sunbury Street, Shamokin, Pa. (5) Agnes Ann Marshall, born August 3, 1830, married first John Letsford, second Joseph Lilley, third Albert Buckingham. With her first husband she had 2 children

and with the second one child. Residence, 1532 Green
Street, Harrisburg, Pa. (6) Theressa Elizabeth Marshall born Oct. 6, 1833 married first Washington Mentz
Silvers, second Richard Thomas Shepherd. With her
first husband she had 3 children and with the second, one
child. Residence, 1504 North Sixth Street, Harrisburg,
Pa.

19. ELIZABETH[1] (John[3], John[2], Christopher[1]).
[Erroneously numbered on page 27.] Born Sept. 14,
1800, married Joseph Riter in 1821 and died May 29,
1855 aged 55 years. Husband died Sept. 1, 1866. They
had seven children : (1) James Monroe Riter, born
Nov. 1821, married Eliza Neely 1869 and died in 1872.
Widow died Dec. 1890. One child, Samuel Neely Riter
was born to them in 1870 who now resides in Pittsburg,
Pa. (2) Delbit Clinton Riter, born Feb. 23, 1825, died
June 30, 1896. Wife is dead and a son Grant Riter resides in Chicago, Ills. (3) Hannah Coleman Riter, married Philip Reymer July 21, 1859, who died in March
1893. Widow resides at No. 17, Bidwell Street, Alle-
gheny, Pa. There were 4 children to this union, (a) Ida
Blanche Reymer, (b) Clement Caughey Reymer, (c) Anna
Elizabeth Reymer, married Roderick Totten, Dec. 1892
to whom was born Elizabeth Riter Totten, Dec. 8, 1893,
(d) Phillip Reymer, Jr., died August 1895. (4) Elizabeth Riter. (5) Margaret Riter, married Jacob Meyers
1870, now resides at Colorado Springs, Colorado. (6)
Thomas Benton Riter married Sophia Ann McCallin April
14, 1875, now reside at No. 5612 Ellsworth Ave., E. E.,
Pittsburg, Pa. They have 4 children : James died Aug.
24, 1892, Mary Alice, Joseph and William Riter, the last
of whom died in June 1890. (7) Iona Rebecca Riter,
married Alexander Andrews of Pittsburg and died Dec.
1880. They had one son Joseph Cummings Andrews.

20. JACOB[4] (Peter[3], John[2], Christopher[1]), born January 2, 1801 in Montgomery county, a physician by profession. He was liberally educated having graduated at

the University of Pennsylvania. He established himself
in the practice of medicine in his native county, but about
1827 located at Selinsgrove, Snyder (then Union) County.
In addition to practicing medicine, he carried on the mercantile business, keeping a general store and dealing exten-
sively in grain. For quite a number of years he was in
partnership with his brother, William F. Wagenseller, in
the old stand at the canal when nearly all the product of
Snyder county was hauled to Selinsgrove. He was thus
engaged at the time of his death which occurred at Selinsgrove April 27, 1847. He had abandoned his profession
some years previously. He was a man of fine business
qualities and made a success in life. He became prominent in public affairs. He was a whig and as such was
elected to the State Senate in which body his intelligence
made him a useful member. He was active in party affairs, and a man of influence in the community, as well as
a leading spirit in every movement calculated to develop
the resources of the county and advance the interests of
Selinsgrove. He served two terms in the Senate, being a
member at the time of his death, representing Juniata,
Mifflin and Union Counties. On January 27, 1829, he
was married by Rev. Daniel Weiser to Mary Richter, born
Dec. 25, 1810, a daughter of Peter Richter, a man who
was prominent and influential about Selinsgrove. Mary
died March 4, 1863. Their union was blessed with eight
children:

+54.   i. Peter Richter[5], born Dec. 8, 1829.

+55.   ii. Sarah Susanna, born Dec 15, 1831.

56.   iii. Lydia Catherine, born Dec. 31, 1833.
Drowned July 1, 1836 at Selins-
grove, Pa.

+57.   iv. Mary Elizabeth, born Feb. 27, 1836.

+58.   v. Benjamin Franklin, born Feb. 17,
1838.

59.   vi. Lydia Catherine, born Oct. 22. 1840,
married William Wagenseller Hol-
man, son of Ann, who was a daugh-

ter of William[3] and Rebecca Wagenseller. (See Number 32, in this
family tree page 37.)

60.   vii. Mattie Virginia, born March 22,
1843, was married to Lloyd Thomas
Sharpless March 5, 1862, by Rev.
Franklin Gearhart. He was born
March 18, 1839 and is a wholesale
and retail Grocer at Bloomsburg,
Pa. Their family record shows 3
children : Benjamin Franklin, born
Feb. 7, 1863, died Feb. 21, 1863 ;
Mary Lillian, born Jan. 14, 1864
and Julia Foster, born May 29,
1879.

61.   viii. John Jacob, born July 16, 1845,
married first March 19, 1872, Mary
A. Willier, born Jan. 23, 1852,
died March 19, 1879. To them
were born two sons, John Carrol
born Sept. 2, 1874, died Nov. 18,
1877 ; Freddie born June 2, 1876,
died Nov. 13, 1877. John was
married second to Clara Hughes,
born March 15, 1851, died Dec.
27, 1891, married third Feb. 15,
1898 to Jennie A. Mears, born Aug.
2, 1862. He resides at Bloomsburg, Pa., and is a traveling salesman.

21.   JOHN[4] (*Peter*[3], *John*[2], *Christopher*[1]), born December 17, 1802 in Montgomery County, Pa. Married
to Mary Ann Norton, Dec. 25, 1823 by Rev. Charles
Moore. She was born September 2, 1805 and died May
19, 1834 while moving from Montgomery County to Columbus Ohio with her husband's father, Peter. He married, second, Catherine Briggs in 1835. She was born
December 8, 1810 in Montgomery County, New York

and after her husband's death, which occurred January 2, 1845, she married (1847) Stacy Taylor. Catherine died March 28, 1853. John was a tailor.

Children, first marriage :

+62. i. Samuel Norton[5], born Feb. 21, 1827.

+63. ii. Araminta, born April 17, 1829.

+64. iii. Mary, born April 14, 1832.

65. iv. Matilda, married first Taylor, second Stephenson of Illinois.

66. v. Sarah Ann, died at the age of 14.

[Among the old family papers there is a record of Susanna died in 1821 or 1827 aged 23 months and 22 days.]

Second marriage :

67. vi. Jacob, born Jan. 8, 1838. About 1863 he went to California for his health. Nothing was ever heard from him and he is supposed to have been killed upon the plains.

68. vii. Emily, born near Columbus, Ohio, Jan. 10, 1840, married William Clemens of Massachusetts May 9, 1865. She died at Columbus, Ohio, of Consumption July 31, 1897. They had 2 children : (1) Catherine Belle, born March 25, 1866 at Pekin, Ills., married Marion T. Henderson of Wellington, N. Y. They have one child Avenel, born Feb. 9, 1886. Residence, Hutchison, Kansas. (2) Allen Briggs, born Feb. 2, 1869, a life insurance agent, resides 595 Bryden Road, Columbus, Ohio.

69. viii. John, born March 29, 1845 and died at Columbus, O. in 1867 of Consumption hastened by exposures in the Civil war.

70.   ix.   George, born ———. Died at the
age of 19 years.

22. CATHERINE⁴, (*Peter³, John², Christopher¹*),
born November 29, 1804 in Montgomery County, married
first Matthew Chain, who died in Franklin County, near
Columbus, Ohio, March 1835. He was the son of Old
Matthew Chain. She married second Elijah Timbrel and
died at Pekin, Illinois in 1872 of Cancer in the breast.
With her first husband she had 4 children and 2 with the
second : (1) William P., who resides in Kansas and has
4 children, Ida, William, John and Charles. (2) Joshua
Wagenseller, is said to be living at Byron, Ogle Co., Ills.
His wife died 1893. (3) Kate and (4) Matilda. Second marriage : (5) John drowned at Memphis, Tennessee while serving his country in the War of the Rebellion. (6) Benjamin, died Dec. 1, 1861 with the measles,
at Jefferson City, Missouri, while serving in the army.

23. HANNAH⁴,(*Peter³, John², Christopher¹*), born
April 25, 1807, married William Hamilton Chain, a
brother of Matthew, who married Hannah's sister, Catherine, above given. They were married March 1, 1831.
William was born August 19, 1809 and died in Franklin
County, Ohio, October 8, 1855. Hannah died May 20,
1880 at Lewistown, Illinois. To them were born six children: (1) Sarah Susanna, born Dec. 27, 1830. She
married Dr. Clinton C. Fisher of Jacksonville, Ills., in
1858. They moved to Los Angelos, California where they
both since died, he Feb. 10, 1893 and she Feb. 10, 1897.
They had 5 children of whom Willie, Charles and Florence
are dead. Walter E. and Harry reside at Los Angelos.
The former is a ship surgeon running to South America.
(2) Theodore Hamilton Chain, born Oct. 30, 1833, died
May 22, 1852. (3) Mary Ann Chain, born August 26,
1836. Married Westy F. Criss, March 4, 1856. He is
a hotel keeper at Carthage, Illinois. They have no issue.
(4) Jacob Matthew Chain, born July 2, 1836, married
Amelia Frances Simms, Feb. 26, 1862. They have six
children of whom Amelia and Frank R. are dead and

Frank Simms, Myrtle, Leo and Ray are living with their parents at Utica, Nebraska. (5) William Hamilton Chain, born, June 13, 1841, married Nellie Smith and died March 16, 1887 at Bushnell, Illinois, where the widow, aged 55, and their children Nelle H. and Charles C. now reside. The latter is publisher of the McDonough *Democrat*, at Bushnell. (6) James Albert Chain, born Dec. 22, 1847 and about 1873 married Nelle Henderson of Indianapolis. They resided in Denver, Colorado and had no children. Both Albert and Nellie were drowned in the China Sea, October 12, 1892 between the island Formosa and the Main land in the wreck of the Bokhara. Nearly all on board perished. Albert was in poor health ; in the hope of improving it, they were making a tour of two years around the world, when unfortunately they were shipwrecked in the storm. Nellie was a fine artist, made many sketches, landscapes, etc. and sold them to Prang for Chromos. Some of her oil paintings sold as high as $800.00 a piece.

24. BENJAMIN[4], (*Peter*[3], *John*[2], *Christopher*[1]), born Nov. 4, 1809, married July 20, 1842 Elizabeth Doyle, who was born August 9, 1826. He died at Pekin, Illinois, March 15, 1844 and left one son :

+71.   i.   Theodore L.[5], born April 18, 1843.

25. JOSHUA[4], (*Peter*[3], *John*[2], *Christopher*[1]), born July 5, 1813 in Providence Township, Montgomery Co., Pa. Married Harriet Rupert, May 1, 1840. She was born July 26, 1823, a descendant of Prince Rupert, who was a prominent man of the Royal family during Cromwell's time and died March 17, 1873. Joshua died at Pekin, Illinois, July 21, 1882. He was a prominent man in his day. He was offered a position in President Lincoln's Cabinet. We shall give a more complete sketch of his life in another part of this book. Joshua and Harriet left a family of 5 children :

+72.   i.   Albert Elon[5], born Feb. 1, 1841.
- 73.   ii.   William Henry, born Feb. 1, 1845.

74. iii. Benjamin, born Jan. 6, 1847, and died Feb. 6, 1848.

75. iv. Laura Catherine, born Nov. 28, 1849, married Algeia Parker in 1870 from whom she is now divorced. Algelia Parker is the only brother of Mrs. Robert G. Ingersoll, the wife of the noted Infidel. Mrs. Parker resides at 3608 Ellis Ave., Chicago, Ills. She has a daughter, Daisy, born Feb. 8, 1871 who in 1890 married William Trimmer, and they too reside in Chicago.

+76. v. Frank Rupert, born Dec. 30, 1851. Joshua and Harriet had six other children now deceased. Minnie born March 30, 1854 and died April 20, 1863 ; Josephine, born Jan. 2, 1857, died March 4, 1858; Alice, born Feb. 26, 1858 and died March 5, 1858; Lida, born, Aug. 21, 1859, died Dec. 9, 1863 ; Harriet M., born Dec. 16, 1861, married March 7, 1878 to D. W. Rider and in 1885 to Gideon Alexander. She died Jan. 5, 1888 at Indianapolis, Indiana. She had one child, Hattie Rider with her first husband, born April 3, 1880 and died 1886 ; Charles Grant Wagenseller born Aug. 10, 1864 and died Feb. 28, 1873.

27. WILLIAM FINDLEY[4] (*Peter*[3], *John*[2], *Christopher*[1]), born Nov. 15, 1817 in Montgomery County, Pa. Went to Columbus, Ohio, with his father in 1834, but soon returned to Selinsgrove, where he engaged in business with his brother Dr. Jacob. He represented Snyder County in the State Legislature and died Aug. 10, 1876. The

Middleburgh *Post*, then published by Hon. Jeremiah Crouse, under date of August 24, 1876. says: "Col. Wm. F. Wagenseller died at his residence in Selinsgrove last Wednesday. Col. Wagenseller was one among the leading business men of the county and much esteemed by all for his fair-dealing and conscientious regard for truth and honesty. He was a man of liberal education, rare business qualifications and sound judgment. As a man of means he always contributed liberally to every charitable and religious purpose. He was one of the pillars of the church—a conscientious, exemplary Christian gentleman. He represented Snyder County in the Legislature and was esteemed as an able legislator. He was one of those men who always had a due deference for the opinions of others and only exacted the same for his own. He was a positive man and those who sustained business relations with him knew precisely how they stood. He was sociable, courteous and dignified. We have lost a valuable citizen and we deeply sympathize with the bereaved relations." Among his descendants we note five children:

+77.   i.   William Jeremiah[5], born Mar. 23, 1839.

+78.   ii. Martin Luther, born Sept. 6, 1840.

79.   iii. Ada E., born June 17, 1842, never mrrried and resides with her mother at Selinsgrove, Pa.

80.   iv. Benjamin Newton, born Oct. 17, 1846, died 1863 of lock jaw, aged 17 years.

81.   v.   Alice Laura, born March 12, 1849, married June 22, 1876, Rev. Emanuel Benton Killinger who was born March 9, 1848 and now resides at Trenton, N. J. No issue.

Col. Wagenseller was married to Amelia Bergstresser, who was born June 26, 1816 and is still residing in Selinsgrove, Pa.

31.   GEORGE[4], (*William*[3], *John*[2], *Christopher*[1]), born

Aug. 17, 1812, never married, was a member of the House of Representatives at Harrisburg from Schuylkill County elected by the democrats. He was one of the three Democrats to vote for Simon Cameron, a Republican, for the United States Senatorship from Pennsylvania. Simon Cameron and the Wagensellers of that period were very fast friends. It was through Joshua Wagenseller of Pekin that Simon Cameron was appointed to a place in President Lincoln's Cabinet. Another evidence that the Cameron-Wagenseller esteem was great lies in the fact that George's brother, John N., named a son in honor of the United States Senator. At the time the subject of the three Democrats voting for Cameron, was widely discussed and is still well remembered over the State. In 1892 the writer was asked by one of the most prominent men of Philadelphia whether that Wagenseller who voted for Cameron was any relation to him [the writer]. We of course plead ignorance, not having known anything about the occurrence. This conversation is recalled only to show what prominence the matter attained at the time. Hon. A. B. Longaker, a nephew of Peter Wagenseller's wife, was a member of the House when the event occurred in 1857. He writes concerning it as follows: "George Wagenseller was a member of the House from Schuylkill County and his colleague was Lebo. I was a member of the House in 1857 and acted as teller upon the part of the House when Cameron was elected over Forney by the votes of three Democrats, Maneer of York, Lebo and Wagenseller. Page 5, of House Journal of 1857 gives the roll of members and page 51, the votes in joint convention. I was a member of the House during the session of 1856 and Speaker of the House in 1858. I know nothing of the details of the life of George Wagenseller of Schuylkill County. He was of dark complexion, dark, if not black hair, strong physical structure, about 6 feet, 2 inches tall, large square chest, somewhat of the cast of an Indian, good-sized head, prominent but rather heavy nose, either gray or dark eyes, weight about 215 to 225 pounds with no extra flesh, but

had a strong and powerful muscular development." At
one time he was Superintendent of a Division of Sunbury
and Erie Railroad and resided at Sunbury. He died Dec.
15, 1873.

33. JOHN NEILOR[4], (*William*[8], *John*[2], *Christopher*[1]), born April 11, 1817, married Sarah McVeigh, who
who died September 26, 1863. They lived at Tamaqua,
Pa., but later, about 1852, moved to Pekin, Illinois, where
they lived four years then went to Sing Sing, New York.
He spent the last 15 years of his life in the hotel business.
He died Feb. 27, 1881. They had 4 children :

82.	i.	James[5], born Jan. 4, 1851, never married, died March 7, 1889.
+83.	ii.	Simon Cameron, born Aug. 13, 1852.
+84.	iii.	George, born Aug. 28, 1862.
85.	iv.	Sarah Elizabeth, born July 31, 1865, resides at Shamokin, Pa.

34. JOHN SCHRACK[4], (*Jacob*[3], *John*[2], *Christopher*[1]), born Nov. 6, 1808, married to Margaret Wynn,
who was born in 1810 and died May 17, 1889, aged 79
years. They had no children. Since printing the notice
of Jacob, John Schrack's father, we learn that he died
about 1852 or 1854 of Dropsy caused by heart and kidney
trouble. He owned a large farm, but he did no work, as
he was a retired gentleman. Jacob was born in Chester
County, Pennsylvania.

35. DAVID SCHRACK[4], (*Jacob*[3], *John*[2], *Christopher*[1]), born April 16, 1812 in Chester County, Pa. He
was married twice, first Sept. 11, 1834 to Ann Myers
Wynn with whom he had ten children, and second to
Hannah McCracken with whom he had no issue. He
was a contractor and builder and died in 1873. The lineage of David follows :

+86.	i.	Martha[8], born Jan. 14, 1836.
+87.	ii.	Mary, born June 16, 1837.
+88.	iii.	Margaret Ann, born Oct. 7, 1840.
+89.	iv.	Levi, born Oct. 4, 1842.

90.   v.   John Ellis, born March 26, 1844,
                  married Mary Lentz of Montgom-
                  ery County.   Residence, Roxbor-
                  ough, Philadelphia, Pa.   To them
                  were born six children.   Only one
                  survives, Mary Della, born Jan. 16,
                  1870, married June 3, 1896 to
                  Harry C. Martin of Roxborough,
                  Phila.   They have one daughter,
                  Mary Della Martin.

+91.   vi. Harriet, born April 2, 1845.

92.   vii. Frances Rebecca, born Dec. 29,
                  1847 and died of Dysentery, Sept.
                  21, 1851.

+93.   viii. James, born Jan. 1, 1849.

94.   ix. Fannie, born Dec. 7, 1852, at New-
                  ton Square, Pa., married July 5,
                  1868 to Harry G. Mason, a son of
                  John D. and Sarah L. Mason.   Har-
                  ry was born in Chester County,
                  June 4, 1846.   They have one child,
                  Mary Ellen, born April 19, 1869,
                  married June 28, 1891 to Robert
                  Birkmere, formerly of the Falls of
                  the Schuylkill.   Harry G. Mason
                  is a hotel proprietor at Eighth and
                  Morton Ave., Chester, Pa.

95.   x.   Bertha, born Sept. 24, 1857, mar-
                  ried July 16, 1870 to Edward Ri-
                  ley of Chester, Pa.   They have
                  three children, Margaret Annie Ri-
                  ley, born July 15, 1885, graduated
                  from Chester High School 1897
                  and from Normal School in June
                  1898, Fanny Mason Riley, born
                  Sept. 1, 1882, a high school student
                  and Harvey Pierce Mallison Riley
                  born Jan. 7, 1885 and died of

Membranous Croup, Mar. 19, 1891.

37. LEVI[4], (*John*[3], *Jacob*[2], *Christopher*[1]), born in Chester County, Pa., married to Catherine Worthington. The Worthingtons in this country are descendants of noble English ancestry, two of them having settled up East and one in Maryland. Both are dead. They had two children. Levi fell down stairs and died from injuries sustained.

+96.   i. John, born March 27, ——.
97.   ii. Daughter, now deceased.

38. SARAH[4], (*Jacob*[3], *John*[2], *Christopher*[1]), married James Pearson with whom she had ten children including twins. Among them are Mrs. Hannah Ann Woodwart of Marshaltown, Pa., Mrs. Emilene Aiken of Honeybrook and Samuel Pearson of near Downingtown.

39. MARGARET[4] (*Jacob*[3], *John*[2], *Christopher*[1]), married James Montgomery, with whom she had two children, Retta Montgomery and Dr. John Montgomery, a successful physician, who now resides in Chambersburg, Franklin County, Pa.

40. MARTHA[4], (*Jacob*[3], *John*[2], *Christopher*[1]), born 1818, married to William McCarraher, formerly a resident of West Chester, died 1884. No issue.

41. ELIZABETH[4], (*Jacob*[3], *John*[2], *Christopher*[1]), born Sept. 2, 1820, married in 1842 to John Donovan, who was born in 1820 and died in 1865, aged 45 years. Elizabeth died November 20, 1891 at Delaware, Ohio, aged 71 years. They had nine children (1) Ellousia, born Feb. 22, 1845, married John Olney Aug. 22, 1867. Residence, Delaware, Ohio. (2) Sarah, born Nov. 25, 1846, died Sept. 9, 1854. (3) Taylor, born Nov. 20, 1848, married Ida Mason Sept. 20, 1881, residence, Sunbury, O. (4) Levi, born Oct. 9, 1850, and died Sept. 3, 1859. (5) Martha Emma, born Sept. 21, 1852, married Thomas S. Clark Oct. 31, 1877. Residence, 137 North Union Street, Delaware, O. Thomas Clark was born Jan. 13, 1850 in South Boston, Massachusetts. Their children are Harry Webster, born April 27, 1878; Flor-

ence Gail, born May 16, 1880; Thomas Herbert, born
Sept. 15, 1882; Martha Pearl, born Nov. 15, 1884 and
Francelia Grace, born July 20, 1887. (6) Mary Isabella, born Oct. 29, 1854, married Charles L. Giviner. Residence, Delaware, O. (7) John Donovan, born May 5,
1856, unmarried, address, Delaware, Ohio. (8) Thomas
Jefferson, born April 2, 1860, married Elizabeth Witt-
linger May 27, 1886, residence, Delaware, O. (9) Harry,
born July 7, 1862, married Carrie Giviner, residence,
Delaware, Ohio.

42.　JOHN CAVENDER⁵, (*George⁴*, *John³*, *John²*,
Christopher¹), born July 24, 1813, married Jane Rebel
and died in September 1870 near Rolla, Missouri. He
used to live in Crawford County, Illinois. His brother,
Amos Wagonseller, Solomon, Kansas, reports that John C.
had six cdildren, three sons and three daughters, as follows :

98.　　　i.　David⁶, born Nov. 24, 1845.
99.　　　ii.　William is married and has two
　　　　　　　children.
100.　　iii.　George.
101.　　iv.　Leticia, married to Howard Mills
　　　　　　　and died soon after.
102.　　v.　Nancy married William Wager, no
　　　　　　　issue.
103.　　vi.　Isabel, married Albert Williams,
　　　　　　　no children.

43.　THOMAS WEIDNER⁵, (*George⁴*, *John³*, *John²*,
Christopher¹), born Nov. 19, 1815, and in September 1849,
was married to Jane Montgomery. He died April 20,
1865. It is supposed that he too lived in Crawford Co.,
Illinois. He had three sons and one daughter. They are :

+104.　　i.　James K.⁶, born July 17, 1850.
105.　　ii.　Robert P., born Aug. 11, 1852,
　　　　　　　married first to Nancy Gaines and
　　　　　　　second to a Miss Johnson. With
　　　　　　　his first wife he had a child
　　　　　　　who died in infancy.

106.	iii.	⎧ Martha, born Jan. 29, 1855.
	Twins.	⎨
107.	iv.	⎩ William J., born Jan. 29, 1855.
108.	v.	John D., born Oct. 10, 1857 and died Oct. 1, 1861.
109.	vi.	Albert C., born July 29, 1862 and died April 15, 1876.

44. ABRAM[5], (*George[4], John[3], John[2], Christopher[1]*), born September 2, 1818, married Barbara McGowen. Abram is still living at Indian Camp Guernsey Co., Ohio. In September, 1898, if he lives, he will be 80 years old. Now he is the oldest living Wagenseller upon the American continent. None of the Wagensellers have ever lived to be very old. Among the oldest was William (11) page 37, who was more than 90 years old when he died. We have made a desperate effort to get a letter from Abram or his family, but we could not accomplish it. The Postmaster at Cambridge, the county seat of Guernsey Co., says, " Abram comes occasionally to this place to transact business. He lives at Indian Camp, this county. " Abram and Barbara had six children, three sons and three daughters :

110.	i.	George[6], born May 8, 1845 (single.)
111.	ii.	John, resides at Indian Camp, O.
112.	iii.	Stephen, married, has two children.
113.	iv.	Elizabeth, born May 24, 1843.
114.	v.	Nancy.
115.	vi.	Leticia.

45. WILLIAM[5], (*George[4], John[3], John[2], Christopher[1]*), born in Beaver county, Pa., June 24, 1821, was married first Feb. 4, 1844 at Palestine, Illinois to Elizabeth Waldrop, who was born Feb. 3, 1818 and died March 4, 1864 while William was in the war. He was married second July 30, 1865, to Eliza A. Gomer and now resides at Hamilton, Missouri. He was the captain of Co. F., Fifth Illinois Cavalry. While he was in the army his father, his mother, his wife and one brother died. At the age of 14 young William left home and went to the far

West.   He returned to Crawford County, Illinois in 1841.
He is now 77 years of age.   He had nine children, six
with the first wife and three with the second wife, as follows:
   First marriage.

116.   i.   Louisa⁶, born July 16, 1845, died
               May 17, 1856.

+117.   ii.   Thomas Harlan, born July 7, 1847.

118.   iii.   Allen, born, Feb. 14, 1849 and
               died March 4, 1856.

119.   iv.   Mary E., born Nov. 9, 1851, in
               Illinois, married May 1, 1875 to
               Daniel Coahran, now reside at Bur-
               bank, Los Angelos Co., California.
               They have three children (1) Wil-
               liam Thomas Clifford Coahran, born
               Feb. 21, 1876, died Aug. 11, 1877.
               (2) Leon Carl Coahran, born June
               21, 1879 and died Aug. 31, 1880.
               (3) Walter Harlan Coahran, born
               August 16, 1883.

120.   v.   Jo. D., born May 30, 1853, is un-
               married and resides at Robinson,
               Crawford Co., Ills.

121.   vi.   Martha, born June 11, 1825, died
               Oct. 6, 1856.

   Second marriage :

122.   vii.   George M., born July 17, 1866 is
               unmarried and when last heard from
               was in Indian Territory.

123.   viii.   Elender Pearl, born June 4, 1868
               and died Oct. 16, 1894.

124.   ix.   Jessie, born March 11, 1872, re-
               sides at home and teaches school.

   46.   AMOS⁵, (George⁴, John³, John², Christopher¹)
born March 30, 1824.   He was married three times, first,
Sept. 24, 1848, to Malinda Rich, who was born June 4,
1827 and died Nov. 29, 1856.   Second, Sept. 6, 1857

to Jemima Snapp, who was born Dec. 12, 1830 and died
Sept. 29, 1872. Third, Sept. 26, 1874 to Elizabeth Rog-
ers, who was born June 14, 1843. Residence Solomon,
Kansas. He is the father of 14 children, 4 with the first
wife, 6 with the second and 4 with the third. To him we
are indebted for the list of the descendants of George Wagenseller of the "Wabash" The descendants of Amos and
of his brothers John C. and Thomas, spell their name with
an "o", thus : "Wagonseller." Amos was born in Beaver County, Pennsylvania and when he was only eighteen
months old, his father moved to Guernsey County, Ohio.
When he was fourteen years old, his father emigrated
farther West and settled in Crawford County, Illinois.
When our subject had lived eighteen or twenty months in
Illinois and had been sick most of the time, he returned to
Ohio, where he remained until he reached his majority.
He then went back to Illinois and worked for his father
on a farm. Having found farming rather uninteresting,
he turned his attention to fast horses and became quite a
sport. Finding that he could neither drink nor swear
very copiously, he became dissatisfied with that kind of a
life and parted with his fast stock. He bought a farm,
was married and settled down to farming and stock raising. During the winter he spent much of his time teaching school. Those were happy days for him ; he had a
good wife, an excellent farm, plenty of stock and some
children. But there were dark days ahead, for after having been married only nine years his wife became ill and
passed to her eternal home, leaving him alone with four
small children, two daughters and two sons. In the necessity of the occasion he married again, sold his farm
and moved to Indiana. He had a neighbor who was Dep-
uty Sheriff. The latter was taken sick and was unable to
attend to his official duties. The papers were placed into
Amos' hands to serve, which led him right into the Sheriff's office and continued in service there for five years.
After his services as Sheriff were no longer required, he
served for several years as County Assessor. Then seeing

a splendid opportunity, he hired several men and opened a carriage and wagon shop. He was a natural genius himself and soon became an efficient workman in wood. On Sept. 29, 1872, he had the misfortune of losing his second wife. In 1877, the Texas boom gave him the fever to go down to the cow boys, and consequently moved down there where he remained for ten years. During the last three years of his stay with our Texas brethren, the weather was very dry, times became very hard, and he, with many others, left the State. Finding himself out of employment he again turned his attention to teaching school. Salaries paid were small and this provided for him only a scant living. Realizing that prospects were not very good, in 1877, he moved to Kansas with only $2.65 in his pocket. His three links (Odd Fellowship) introduced him into good society and brought him plenty of work as a carpenter. His life seemed to have been marked off in periods and it was about time for him to have another misfortune. On the very day that Corbet and Fitzsimmons battled for the championship of the world, his house was entirely consumed with fire and everything lost but the beds, clothing and furniture. The accumulation and the fruits of eight years of industry and of toil was swept from him in a single hour, as he had no insurance. Things looked very gloomy for awhile, but his good friends, the members of the Odd Fellows, came to his relief. While they gave him substantial aid they did not restore him to where he was before the fire. He had been in substantial circumstances two or three times, but in his old age, he finds himself with but little of this world's goods. He is now (1898) seventy-four years old, too old, he thinks to make another raise. A letter to the writer, he closes by saying, " Life has been a failure, " meaning, of course, his own. In this we fail to agree with our aged relative. It certainly was not as pleasant as his many friends would wish it to have been, but there is no one, we verily believe, reading these lines, who will say that his life has been a failure. The children of Amos are as follows:

First marriage.

125.   i.   Dora⁶, born Aug. 13, 1849, married to Stephen Wortman, who died Oct. 2, 1889, aged 41 years, 6 months and 21 days. Dora died Dec. 21, 1881 aged 32 years, 4 months and 8 days. Their home was at Carlisle, Sullivan County, Indiana. To them were born three children : Richard Austin, born Feb. 15, 1874 ; Charles Phillip, born Dec. 17, 1875, died Sept. 8, 1886, and Sarah Elizabeth, born Nov. 6, 1876, now resides at Carlisle, Ind.

126.   ii.   Sarah Elizabeth⁶, born Aug. 22, 1851, married Hubert Eldred and died Sept. 26, 1890. Widower's residence, No. 1538 Liberty Ave., Terre Haute, Ind.

+127.   iii.   William Riley, born Dec. 11, 1853.

128.   iv.   John Martin, born March 26, 1856 in Crawford County, Ills., was married Jan. 23, 1885 to Anna Mills, who was born in Terre Haute, Indiana, June 28, 1871. He is conducting a Drug Store at No. 103 Ohio Street, Terre Haute, Indiana. They have a son, Earl Amos, born Nov. 29, 1895.

Second marriage.

129.   v.   Elizabeth, born June 9, 1858, died March 11, 1860.

130.   vi.   Mattie, born July 31, 1860, was married in October, 1889 to Dr. Charles Combs of Guthry, Indian Territory. They have two children.

131.   vii.   George M., born Dec. 12, 1862,

was married August 20, 1889 to Sallie Preston of Marshall, Illinois. He resides in Solomon, Kansas, where he conducts the business of dealing in Farming Implements. They have a daughter, Irene, born July 16, 1890.

132.	viii.	Charles P., born Nov. 24, 1864, married June 27, 1895 to Cintha W. Root, who was born 1858. He is a Telegraph Operator and Ticket Agent. They have two children, Charles Albert and Amos Sheldon.
133.	ix & x.	Twin Boys, not named, born April 1, 1867 and died April 11, 1867.

Third marriage.

134.	xi.	Ada May, born August 1, 1875 at Oaktown, Ind. and died Jan. 11, 1882.
135.	xii.	Birtis Franklin, born July 14, 1879 and died Jan. 3, 1882.
135.	xiii.	Infant son (twin to Iona) born Mar. 14, 1883 and died Mar. 15, 1883.
137.	xiv.	Iona, born March 14, 1883. Going to school at Solomon, Kansas.

49. JULIA MATILDA⁵, (*Abraham⁴, John³, John², Christopher¹*), born at Lionville, Pa. Dec. 13, 1826, married Dec. 25, 1842 at R. to John Irey of Spring Forge, son of Peter Irey. Julia's husband died Sept. 26, 1893 and the widow now resides at No. 349 Church Street, Phoenixville, Pa. They had a family of eleven children : (1) Henry Meyers Irey, born at Springton Forge, Feb. 19, 1847, was married Jan. 27, 1880 to Nellie Isabella Henderson of Ottawa, Illinois, who was born August 23, 1864 in Lasalle County, Ills. Residence, Genoa, Nebraska. They had nine children. (2) Amanda Catherine Irey, born Nov. 14, 1848 at Springton Forge and died March 9, 1850. (3) Isabella Christian Irey, born June

17; 1850 and died June 25, 1851. (4) George Godard
Irey, born April 23, 1852 at Glen Moore, Chester County,
and was married Dec. 19, 1878 at Morgantown, Berks
County, to Anna Broadbent who was born in 1858. He
resides in Omaha, Nebraska and has a family of three children. (5) Ella Irey, born Jan. 23, 1854 and died Oct.
2, 1855. (6) Annie Meyers Irey, born July 17, 1856
at Isabella Forge, married Oct. 16, 1879 to Kinzer Van
Buskirk, a hardware dealer in Pottstown, Pa., who was
born April 5, 1848. They have 5 children. (7) Horace Beal Irey, born Jan. 1, 1859 at Isabella Forge, married June 28, 1883 to Sarah Chrisman, who was born in
Chester County, 1858. He has been prominent in political
and financial affairs, having been County Treasurer of Omaha, Nebraska, where he, his wife and 2 children now reside.
(8) Ellen J. Irey, born Feb. 12, 1861 at Isabella Forge,
married Feb. 21, 1898 to Mildred Stephenson, who was
born June 21, 1870 in Omaha, Neb. They reside in St.
Louis. He is a Civil Engineer. (9) Lizzie M. Irey,
born August 14, 1864 at Isabella, married March 30,
1892 to Dr. Charles More Benham, a homeopathic doctor,
who was born Sept. 5, 1865 and now resides in Phoenixville, Pa. They have two children. (10) Norman Walter Irey, born Oct. 8, 1868, near Isabella and died Feb. 7,
1888 while attending the Inter-State Commercial College
at Reading, Pa., he became ill suddenly and died within
nine days. (11) Lorena May Irey, born Dec. 19, 1870,
married Oct. 8, 1892 to Walter E. McConnel of Honeybrook, Chester County, Pa. They had three children.
While Mrs. McConnel was on a short visit to her mother
and sister in 1897 at Phoenixville, she was seized with
lock jaw and died June 8th. John Irey, the father of
these children, went West four times. He went west in
1856, 1864, 1882 and 1893. He was a carpenter and followed that trade until 1843. Then he went into the iron
business with Dr. John B. Chrisman of Coventry at Springton Forge. In 1851, he retired for four years. In April
1856 Irey and Butler bought Isabella Forge from David

Potts. They continued the business for several years when Mr. Irey bought Mr. Butler's interest and ran the business alone until 1865 he sold to Levi Smith. Mr. Irey and his wife then moved about a mile away where they lived for 30 years and reared their family. Henry, the eldest son, soon after graduated and took up 1600 acres of land in Western Nebraska. The hard times, drouth and hot winds sometimes was against him. Horace went West in the 80s, first to Illinois then to Omaha, Nebraska, where he has been for some years and became quite prosperous. He was twice elected County Treasurer. Since 1893 the West has not prospered much. The Exposition now in progress in Omaha (June 1898) is expected to give an impetus to business West of the Mississippi River.

50. MARY ELIZABETH⁵, (*Abraham⁴, John³, John², Christopher¹*), born May 3, 1830 at Lionville, Pa. She married Dr. B. G. Miller, who resides at 1509 Second Avenue, Rock Island, Illinois. They have 3 children living and married : (1) George Meyers Miller born March 27, 1852, married July 2, 1878 to Mary E. Diller. They have three children and reside at No. 222 Third Street, Ft. Madison, Iowa. (2) Clara Elizabeth Miller born Dec. 12, 1854, married Dec. 25, 1878 to Alfred J. Taylor of Fremont, Nebraska. They have five children. (3) Benjamin Griffith Miller, born May 4, 1858, married Jan. 25, 1877 to Nellie Karsting. He is the General Foreman of Atchinson, Topeka and Santa Fe Railway Company and resides at 202 Oak St., Ft. Madison, Iowa.

51. THOMAS MEYERS⁵,(*Abraham⁴, John³, John², Christopher¹*), born Aug. 14, 1833 at Lionville, Pa., married April 26, 1862 to Mary Melinda Rice of Perryville. He died Feb. 7, 1871 at Pontiac, Ills. His widow married Richard Stratton, of Peoria, Ills. Thomas had three children :

138.	i.	John Abraham Jesse⁶, born July 18, 1863, died June 14, 1864.
139.	ii.	Juniata Watres, born Aug. 20,

1865, married June 28, 1891 to
John T. Green of Pontiac, Illinois
Two children are recorded to them,
Mabel May, born Nov. 28, 1893
and Francis Fern, born Sept. 22,
1896, died April 5, 1897.

140. iii. Willie Willikson, born March 30,
1867 and died Oct. 11, 1871.

141. iv. Harry Wrye, born Oct. 26, 1868
at Newport, Perry County, Pa.
When he was only a year old his
parents moved to Fairbury, Ills.
He was only a little more than two
years of age when his father died.
At the age of 18 years he went to
North Platte, Nebraska, for his
health and after his health improved, he taught school. He attended
a Business College at Bloomington,
Illinois and afterward followed farming again as it agreed better with
his health. He is now farming a
half section of land and raising
stock. (See Portrait in this work.)
He resides at Fairbury, Livingston
Co., Illinois and has a son John
Richard, born Sept. 6, 1897 to him
and his wife, who was Frances Emma Goold of Woodland, Indiana,
having been married March 7, 1894.

52. JOHN ANDREW⁵, (Abraham⁴, John³, John³,
Christophei¹), born Dec. 11, 1836, married May 18, 1864
to Emily Johnstone. He established a book-printing es-
tablishment and continued it until a year or so ago, compelled to retire to prolong life, he turned the business over
to his son. For many years he has resided at 142 Price
Street, Germantown, Philadelphia, but he has quite recently moved to Pittsburg, Pa. They had six children :

142.   i. William⁶, born June 28, 1865, and died June 30, 1865.

143.   ii. Jane Johnstone, born April 23, 1867, married Nov. 28, 1893 to Sherman Smith a Photo-Engraver, of Pittsburg. They reside at 229 Fairmount Ave., Pittsburg, E. E. Pa. To them have been born two daughters, Edith W., born July 23, 1895 and died July 27, 1895, and Miriam Wagenseller, born Oct. 18, 1896.

144.   iii. Mary Meyers, born June 20, 1869, married Nov. 5, 1891 to William H. Ball, a banker. They reside at 30 East Washington Lane, Germantown, Pa. and have 3 children, Wm. Whitney, born Nov. 16, 1892, Emily Wagenseller, born Aug. 1, 1894 and Frances Dowling, born June 10, 1897.

145.   iv. Eliza Hong, born May 29, 1872 married May 11, 1893 to William H. Whitney, a banker of Philadelphia. Residence, 59 West Johnson Street, Germantown, Pa. They have one child, William Henry Whitney, Jr., born March 4, 1894.

146.   v. Hudson, born May 8, 1874, married Mary Mackie Neilor. He is the successor of his father, who established a commercial and book-printing business in 1860. He is doing business at 31 South Sixth Street, Philadelphia. They have 2 sons, Hudson Harry, born Nov. 7, 1895 and John Andrew, Jr., born Feb. 16, 1898.

147.   vi. John Ray, born Jan. 28, 1878 and
died Sept. 27, 1890.

53. EMILY LAW⁵, (*Abraham⁴, John³, John²*),
Christopher¹), born Dec. 3, 1839 in Uwchlan Township,
Chester County, Pa., married May 7, 1882 to Newton
Smith, merchant of Ulster County, N. Y., who died in
Ottawa, Illinois, Dec. 10, 1884. Widow resides at 217
Second Ave., Peoria, Ills. To them were born 7 children :
(1) Andrew N. Smith, born June 14, 1863, married May
19, 1886 to Alice ———. He is a Wholesale Grocer at
Pontiac, Illinois. (2) Jane Emily, born Dec. 19, 1865,
married June 13, 1888 to Daniel Welpley of New York
City, a traveling salesman. They have one son. (3)
Henry, born Feb. 3, 1868, died Feb. 9, 1868. (4) Wm.
H. Smith, born April 2, 1869, is a cigar manufacturer at
Peoria, Ills. (5) Edwin E. Smith, born June 23, 1872,
is a Hotel keeper at Pontiac, Ills. (6) Jared Miller, born
April 19, 1876, is a Financial Secretary and resides at
Peoria, Ills. (7) Eva A., born Dec. 14, 1881, died
Dec. 17, 1881.

54, PETER RICHTER⁵, (*Jacob⁴, Peter³, John²,
Christopher¹*), born Dec. 8, 1829 in Selinsgrove, Union,
(now Snyder) County, Pennsylvania. In his youth, he devoted his time principally to attending the schools of his
native place, which in that day already were conducted by
earnest and experienced men, In his classes he ranked
high and was noted for his close application to study and
the rapid progress he acquired. At the age of sixteen he
entered the preparatory department of Pennsylvania College at Gettysburg, and graduated with honors from the
said institution in the summer of 1852. Having in the
mean time, given his attention to the study of medicine under the preceptorship of the late Dr. Henry Huber, of
Gettysburg, he, upon his graduation from College, entered
the Medical Department of Pennsylvania College, at Philadelphia and graduated *Medicinae Doctor* in 1858. Upon
receiving his Medical degree, he returned to Selinsgrove,
and commenced the practice of his profession. Here he

remained, engaged in active practice, for a period of twenty years. Dr. P. R. Wagenseller was a faithful and earnest physician. He had a love for his profession, was a close student, and, as a consequence, was always apace with the advancement made in the science of medicine. He frequently contributed articles to the various medical works published in his day, and exhibited in his productions an intelligence and mastery that placed him in the front ranks of his calling. So great was his skill as a physician, and so great the esteem and confidence in which he was held, that his early demise, at the age of 43 years, in the midst of his usefulness and activity, was a source of sincere regret on the part of the community in which he lived. In connection with his practice, he was also for many years a partner with J. G. L. Shindel, in conducting the principal drug-store of the place. On July 19, 1854, he was joined in wedlock to Miss Catherine Chritzman, daughter of George and Mary (nee Ulrich) Chritzman, of Gettysburg.

In addition to the practice of his profession, Dr. Wagenseller occupied from time to time, positions of honor and trust. In 1864, during the Rebellion, he was the examining surgeon of enrollment board of the fourteenth district of Pennsylvania. He afterward became the examining physician on pensions, which appointment he held to the time of his death. At different periods he was a member of the Town Council and was also the Chief Burgess of the Borough of Selinsgrove. In educational matters he took a deep interest, serving as school director in the public schools, and as director of Missionary Institute, now Susquehanna University, Selinsgrove, Pa. At Missionary Institute, he was elected lecturer of Physiology and Hygiene and occupied the same office in the Susquehanna Female College. He was a consistent member of the Lutheran church at different times being an officer of the congregation to which he belonged. By his precept, his example and his means, he was ready to further all good and worthy objects. In life he ranked with the good and useful citizens of the place, and in death, which occurred

August 18, 1873, has left to the public a legacy of good works and Christian example. Dr. Peter Richter and Catherine Wagenseller were the parents of six children :

148.   i.   Mary Amelia[6], born July 18, 1854 and died in infancy.

+149.   ii. Franklin Jacob, born Oct. 8, 1855.

+150.   iii. George C., born June 30, 1857.

151.   iv. Lemisa Albertha, born Dec. 29, 1859, married June 16, 1881 to Dr. B. F. Emerick, a prominent physician and druggist of Carlisle, born in Northumberland County, Nov. 4, 1859. They have an interesting family of three children: (1) Anna Catherine, born March 25, 1882. (2) Paul Wagenseller, born March 11, 1886. (3) Alford Benjamin, born Oct. 6, 1891.

152.   v.   Gertrude A., born Sept. 29, 1861, and died in infancy.

153.   vi. Annie E., born Sept. 2, 1865, married Jan. 19, 1886 to J. Alfred Strohm of Newville, Cumberland County, born March 31, 1859. He is a traveling salesman and resides at Carlisle, Pa. One son, G. Alfred, to them was born March 22, 1895.

55. SARAH SUSANNA[5], (*Jacob*[4], *Peter*[3], *John*[2], *Christopher*[1]), born Dec. 15, 1831, married July 15, 1851 to Jesse Benner Evans of Uwchlan, Chester County, Pa., who was born Oct. 3, 1824. Mr. Evans' mother was Eliza King, daughter of Conrad King and Catherine Wagenseil. (See Chapter on King descendants.) J. B. Evans and Sarah Susanna Wagenseller were the parents of six children: (1) Benjamin Franklin Evans, born July 23, 1851, married June 14, 1877 to Essie E. Guthrie. They have three children, Clarence G., Bessie and Gertrude. Residence, Downington, Pa. (2) Lida E. Evans, born

July 29, 1854, married August 1, 1877, by Rev. Jersey, to Clark Pierson, Editor of the *Record*, Lambertville, N. J. They have two children, Jessie, born June 24, 1880, and Grace, born Jan. 10, 1882. (3) Lewis Wilmer Evans, born Sept. 28, 1856, married Kate Fockler. They have one daughter, Edna G., born Feb. 11, 1886. He is a compositor on the Philadelphia *Public Ledger*. (4) Mattie Evans, born July 2, 1860, married to William W. McKinley Dec. 16, 1832 with whom she had a daughter, Mabel, now deceased. Mrs. McKinley died Dec. 15, 1884. (5) Abbie Evans, born Sept. 20, 1863 died, Nov. 1, 1884. (6) Gertrude Evans, born April 17, 1868 and died Dec. 7, 1884.

57. MARY ELIZABETH[5], (*Jacob[4]*, *Peter[3]*, *John[2]*, *Christopher[1]*), born Feb. 27, 1836 and was baptized Aug. 29th of the same year. She was a child of early religious convictions, was converted at a Methodist Meeting in a school house in Selinsgrove the year following her father's death in 1848. Promises made at the bedside of her dying father hastened this change. She was married to Rev. Franklin Gearhart of Danville, Pa., a Methodist Clergyman on Jan. 13, 1854. Rev. Franklin Gearhart was born, opposite Danville, Pa., June 19, 1821, near what is now called Riverside, on a farm. He was converted in Oct. 1839 at 18 years of age in the old McIntyre Church near Catawissa while escorting his aged grandfather, Jacob Gearhart, a Local Preacher, to the meeting. Jacob Gearhart was also known as Judge Gearhart. Franklin was the son of Jacob Gearhart, and Amelia Housel. His father was known as 'Squire Gearhart. Jacob Gearhart and Amelia Housel were married Dec. 12, 1813. Amelia Housel Gearhart died Oct. 6, 1836. Isabella Gearhart died Dec. 10, 1850. Jacob Gearhart was sent to the Pennsylvania Assembly by the Democratic party. Jacob Gearhart, Jr., Franklin's father, was born March 17, 1893. Amelia Housel Gearhart born March 12, 1762. Franklin was the second son and fourth child. He entered the ministry in 1845, was instrumental in the conversion of at least

DR. P. R. WAGENSELLER,
1829--1873.   [NO. 54.]

3000 souls, died peacefully at Williamsport, Pa., Feb. 1, 1890 and was buried in Selin's Grove. Their children are as follows: (1) Olin Gearhart, born at Mifflintown, Jan. 21, 1855, died Feb. 12, 1855. (2) Edmund Bremen Gearhart, born at McVeytown, Pa., Sept. 7, 1856, was born again, Aug. 1870 at Watsontown, licensed to preach in 1874 and graduated at Dickinson Seminary, Williamsport, Pa., later at Drew Theological Seminary, New Jersey and still later at Syracuse University, New York, afterward taking a degree by study for the degree, Ph.D. Has been an Insurance Agent the past four months. He was married by Rev. F. H. Clark to Miss Alice Estelle Dunham, Sept. 7, 1882, of Bridgeport, New York. They had three children, Grace, born Oct. 29, 1886, died Sept. 9, 1887. David Dunham, born Aug. 8, 1888, in Palmyra, N. Y. and Edmund Bremen, Jr., born May 21, 1892 in Cananduagua, N. Y. Residence, No. 1202 Corbin St., Syracuse, N. Y. (3) Georgia Ridgely Gearhart, born in Selinsgrove, Oct. 3, 1859 and graduated at Wesleyan Female College, Wilmington, Delaware. She married Samuel Lewis Hain of Houston, Texas. He was born in Reading, Pa. They had three children, Martha, born 1886 Louisa, born 1888 and Clarence Gearhart, born 1890, died in 1892. Residence No. 215 West 23d St., New York City. (4) Mary Amelia Gearhart, born in Bloomsburg, Pa., Jan. 1, 1862, died at McEwensville, Oct. 20. 1862 and was buried at Milton. Franklin Swallow Gearhart, born at Catawissa, June 14, 1864, was married in 1892 to Dolly ———. He is now in Alaska. (6) Wilbur Fisk Gearhart, born in Hanover, Pa., June 18, 1868, married Miss Anna Middendorf of Louisville, Ky. She was born Oct. 5, 1859 in Louisville, Ky., where they now reside at 311 West Walnut St. They have no heirs. He has charge of a Gymnasium being a fine Athletic teacher. (7) Lloyd Sharpless Gearhart, born in Watsontown, March, 1, 1872, was married in 1896 in New Orleans to Mrs. Gussie Gresham, who is a New York State woman, born about 1875, no heirs. He is also an Athletic Teacher. Residence, Corner

Sixth Avenue and 59th Street, New York City. Mary Elizabeth's life has been spent in looking after her family and for God and humanity.

58. BENJAMIN FRANKLIN[5], (*Jacob*[4], *Peter*[3], *John*[2], *Christopher*[1]), born Feb. 17, 1838 in Selinsgrove, Union (now Snyder) County, Pennsylvania. In 1851 he became a student in the preparatory department of Pennsylvania College, Gettysburg, and still later he was a student at the University of Lewisburg. Coming from a family distinguished for its medical ability, he, at an early age, turned his attention to his profession, and, in 1856, began reading with Dr. Samuel Wagenseller at Pekin, Ills. During 1858 and 1859, he read with his brother, Dr. P. R. Wagenseller, at Selinsgrove; then he became a student in the medical department of the University of Pennsylvania, Philadelphia, from which he graduated in 1860. In 1861 he opened an office in Beavertown, Snyder County, Pennsylvania, and in August 1862, he was commissioned by Governor Curtin, as Assistant Surgeon of the 139th P. V. I. On January 31st, 1863, he was commissioned Surgeon with rank of Major. In September 1863, he was mustered out with the Regiment. When the 201st Pennsylvania Regiment was ordered out, Dr. Wagenseller was commissioned Surgeon with the rank of Major and so served until the close of the war. Among the difficult duties performed was the burial early in September 1862, by the 139th Regiment of the Union Soldiers who had fallen in the battle of Bull Run about a week before and still lay on the field exposed to the hot summer sun. Most of the Confederate dead had already been interred and the soldiers of the 139th under a flag of truce performed the last sad rites over the neglected bodies of our fallen heroes, burying fifteen hundred in three days.

Since the close of the war, Dr. Wagenseller has been in active practice at Selinsgrove, his character and ability winning him a high rank among his professional brethren. He is a member of the Snyder County Medical Society; of the State of Pennsylvania and the American Medical Association. In the two first named he has served as President. For 25 years he has been surgeon of the Pennsylvania Railroad and at one time he filled the chair of Physiology at Susquehanna University, Selinsgrove. At all times a Republican, he has for many years been identified with the organization of his party and has been a delegate to a number of state conventions and to three national conventions. In 1868 he was an elector and cast his vote for Grant and Colfax. In 1869 he was commissioned by President Grant as Revenue Assessor of the 14th district comprising the counties of Dauphin, Juniata, Northumberland, Snyder and Union and served until 1878. During the following year he was a candidate for the State Senate and during the same year he was appointed Examining Surgeon of the United States Board of Pension Examiners. During 1882 he received the Republican nomination for Congress. In local affairs he has always been extremely active and has officiated as a member of borough council and was several times elected chief burgess. He served as postmaster of Selinsgrove under President Harrison's administration. He has also been identified with business interests to some extent and was formerly a director in the Snyder County Bank. In the new telephone company which erected lines in Snyder County during 1897, he superintended the construction of the line and is now one of the leading directors of the concern. In religious faith he is a Lutheran and since early manhood he has been a member of the church. Socially he is connected with the Masonic Order as a member of Lafayette Lodge. On March 25, 1861, he was married to Maria A. Schoch, daughter of Jacob Schoch, and he has only one child, Martha Jeneatte, born August 18, 1862, who on Oct. 1, 1885 married Martin L. Snyder. The result of this union is a daughter, Marie, born Aug. 19, 1887. Mr. Snyder has been studying Theology and is now completing his course at Susquehanna University. He has been called to Bedford, Bedford County, Pa., to fill the pulpit of the Luth-

eran church of that place. Dr. Wagenseller is a leading
physician of Selinsgrove, a man of ability and has through
force of character become prominent and has come to the
front as a leader of men.

62. SAMUEL NORTON[5], (*John[4]*, *Peter[3]*, *John[2]*,
Christopher[1]), was born Feb. 21, 1827. He was married
and had two daughters and one son. He resides at Ukiah,
California, and in a letter dated Jan. 6, 1898, he says that
his wife and children are all dead. He has two grand-
children living.

63. ARAMINTA[5], (*John[4]*, *Peter[3]*, *John[2]*, *Christopher[1]*), born Apr. 14, 1829, married March 14, 1850 to
Reuben Bergstresser who was born in Selinsgrove Jan. 9,
1824 and died in Denver, Colorado, May 10, 1888, of
apoplexy. Araminta died in Pekin, Illinois, of typhoid
pneumonia, Jan. 25, 1861. Reuben Bergstresser is a brother of Amelia Bergstresser married to William F. Wagenseller, now deceased, (see No. 27, page 53). Reuben
and Araminta had four children, two are living and two
are dead : (Ida Bell Bergstresser, born Dec. 30, 1850,
married Sept. 27, 1871 to John Anthony Jones, who was
born August 10, 1846. He is a real estate agent and
loan broker in Bloomington, Illinois. They have six children, (a) Frank Edgar Jones, born August 4, 1872, is now
in the scientific department of the American Lucifer Prism
Co., at No. 1127, "The Rookery," Chicago. He left the
North-western University in February 1897 to accept the
position, thereby cutting himself off 3 months' short of
graduation. (b) Albert Reuben Jones, born Sept. 14,
1874, is in the class of '99 at the North-western University, Evanston, Illinois and will be a disciple of Blackstone.
(c) Flora B. Jones, born Dec. 15, 1876, is a student of
Wesleyan University, Bloomington, Illinois. (d) Harry
Wagenseller Jones, born 22, 1879, a student of the high
school, gathers news and inclines to journalism. (e) Roy
Bergstresser Jones, born Sept. 19, 1884, and (f) Clara
Burnell Jones, born Jan. 29, 1889. (2) Edgar P. Berg_

R. F. Wagenseller

stresser, born Nov. 7, 1853 and died March 21, 1873. He was killed by the accidental discharge of a gun he had in his buggy while driving from Pekin, Illinois, to visit Spring Lake on a hunting expedition. (3) Flora Bergstresser, born Aug. 6, 1858, married James Mills Burnell, who was born Oct, 9, 1851. They have two children, Jennette Louise, born May 2, 1886 and Ruth Marguerite, born May 9, 1888. They reside at 1658 Humboldt Street, Denver, Colorado. Mr. Bunnel is business manager of the "Rocky Mountain News." He bought one-third interest in the paper in 1886 and later increased his stock to one-half ownership. In 1891 he sold out his interest, but since then he has been induced to again accept the position of business manager. (4) Frank Bergstresser, born Dec. 30, 1860 and died August 20, 1861.

64. MARY⁵, (*John⁴, Peter³, John², Christopher¹*), born April 14, 1832, married three times, first to John Taylor Perkins, who died May 12, 1852, second in 1854 to William Scott Rankin of Monrovia, California, who was born in 1816 and died Oct. 29, 1890, aged 84 years, third, on June 9, 1897, to Lewis Lutz of East Las Vegas, New Mexico. She is the mother of four children, one with the first husband and three with the second. (1) Annie Josephine Perkins was born May 2, 1852 in Pekin, Illinois, married Nov. 19, 1873 to Milton Randolph Moore of Tepeka, Kansas, who was born Sept. 27, 1846 at Summitville, Indiana. They now reside at Arizola, Pinal County, Arizona. Mr. Moore is a war invalid having been shot through the right lung, Oct. 8, 1864 when but 18 years old. He was a member of the House of Representatives from Pinal County in 1894. He is a journalist by profession. They have had five children: (a) Thomas, born in Topeka, Kansas, Aug. 30, 1874, died in Chicago, Illinois, March 23, 1890 and was buried at Monrovia, California, March 29, 1890. (b) Eda Viola, born Oct. 22, 1876 in Topeka, Kansas, married July 7, 1896 at Florence, Arizona, to George E. Sanders, of Arizola, Arizona. (c) Kirk Tonner, born Oct. 4, 1882 at Topeka, Kansas. (d) Roy Webb,

born May 20, 1884, at Topeka and (e) Nino, born Nov. 11, 1885 at Topeka. (2) Lizzie Rankin, born 1857, married to P. C. Carpenter of Las Vegas, New Mexico, who was born in 1849. No issue. (3) Algernon Sydney Rankin, born Aug. 25, 1859, married Nora Norris, who was born 1848. They reside in Topeka, Kansas. (4) Mary Edo Rankin, born 1863, married Sept. 21, 1885 to C. F. Moore of Monrovia, California, where they now reside. They have two children, Algernon, who is dead and Sidney H., born July 6, 1894. Mary Rankin Lutz is endowed with more than the usual amount of intelligence and mental vigor. She is the author of many brilliant and touching poems. She is five feet, two inches tall and weighs 135 pounds. Her husband has weighed 265 pounds, but has been reduced to 189 pounds. He is of German descent and has four children, all married, and three grand children. The author can not refrain from quoting from Mrs. Lutz's letter: "I think that married life is just what we make it ourselves and now we want to get all the good out of the lottery of life and as we journey toward the setting sun and approach the end, we hope to find more of the beautiful and the good. The world is as beautiful now as it has been, life is as sweet and flowers bloom as fair as when I was young." On the very day she was sixty years of age, surrounded by the solitude and loneliness of widowhood and having thrust upon her the unwelcome thought that not even a child of hers was in the state, under such circumstances, she penned the letter we publish below. The thoughts expressed are characteristic of her life, hence we deem no apology necessary for the introduction of this letter as a portion of her sketch. The letter is as follows :

MRS. LUTZ'S LETTER.

WRITTEN WHEN SIXTY YEARS OF AGE.

"My Dear Friend.—The Calender says I am sixty to-day. I have passed the half milestone and left it behind on my way. Am I old? Do you ask ? Why no. My heart is still young. My limbs they grow tired sometimes and are not very young, I look back on this journey of life and dim vista of years. I still see the sunshine, the shadows, the smiles and the tears, and the face of one dead cut down in his vigor and prime, before he reached life's spring or early summer time, and one just as dear who reached his three score years and ten. He loved me, with all my faults, he was one of the best of men. Each one formed a link in the chain of my very life and heart, but God wills that, sooner or later, all loved ones must part. I can still see the bended knee and fairy little faces, who once knelt at my side in their accustomed places. Then when their evening prayers were said, and kisses, two and three, were given, they were tucked in bed as warm as could be. Now girls and boys stand before me grown to be women and men. It is then human nature asserted herself over and over again. Each one loved another and went out to other homes. That is why I sit here so quiet, so still and alone. Do not think I wish to repine to murmur, or even complain, I would not, if I could, call either one back to this home nest again. All have been happily married and all are contented in life, and I do not regret that I have been made mother or wife. The only regret that I have, is we live so far apart, I so long for dear Edo's baby, to love and press to my heart, and sing him the songs, I sung to her mother long ago, when I hushed her to sleep in the twilight and played her peek-a-boo. How sweet to remember those precious times, when I lulled each one to rest. Those tender babes, how I loved each one as they lay upon my breast! My children call me blessed, and always do remember, when all my birthdays come, as well the twenty-fifth of December, and children's children being to us the link that in life's chain quite stays with me sometimes because he thinks he must be only 8 years old but can sing, play the piano and many other things, still how can I help to think of dear hands and voices I loved to touch and hear? They are all away from my side to-night, and I only hear the echo. Only two years ago to-day, we two sat here alone, my hand was softly folded in one forever gone. And we sat like two silly

children, just like when we were young. We talked of
birthdays, wedding days came in for a share, we thanked
the Lord for His goodness, His kindness and loving care."
Mrs. Lutz's life and character is interesting to study and
an honor to those who gave her being.

71. THEODORE L.[5], (*Benjamin[4]*, *Peter[3]*, *John[2]*,
Christopher[1]), born April 18, 1843, married at Chillicothe,
Illinois, Sept. 6, 1866 to Emilie Lander, who was born
August 30, 1845. He resides at No. 645 Everett Ave.,
Kansas City, Kansas. Theodore was but an infant when
his father died and Joshua Wagenseller, his uncle, cared
for him. He was a Soldier in the late War. They are
the parents of six children :

154.   i.   Allen Lawrence[6], born in Chilli-
                 cothe, Ills. June 22, 1867. Resi-
                 dence, Kansas City, Kansas.
155.   ii. Harry Lander, born Nov. 3, 1870,
                 married May 11, 1897 to Leonora
                 Hill, who was born in New Or-
                 leans, Louisiana, Feb. 22, 1876.
156.   iii. Ernest Elmer, born Dec. 11, 1872
                 and died Nov. 19, 1878.
157.   iv. John Charles, born March 15, 1875,
                 died July 28, 1876.
158.   v.   Clara Alice,   ⎫
159.   vi. Clarence Clay, ⎬ Twins, born Oct.
                           ⎭
                 22, 1879. Residence, Kansas City,
                 Kansas. [While compiling this
                 history the author has had the pleas-
                 ure of receiving from Miss Clara
                 Alice, an invitation to attend the
                 graduation exercises of the Kansas
                 City High School, May 26, 1898
                 of which she is a member.]

72. ALBERT ELON[5], (*Joshua[4]*, *Peter[3]*, *John[2]*,
Christopher[1]) ,born Feb. 1, 1841, was married to Mary E.
Hammer at the home of the bride in Pekin, Illinois, by
Rev. E. P. Livingston, March 27, 1873. They are now

HARRY W. WAGENSELLER,
FAIRBURY, ILLINOIS.

divorced. She was married Feb. 24, 1897 to Hubbard Sylvester Latham. Albert was a soldier in the late war and now resides at Manito, Illinois. The issue of Albert and Mary are five children :

160.	i.	Laura May, born Aug. 25, 1876, married Sept. 30, 1896 to Charles Peniel, Operator, Jerseyville, Ills.
161.	ii.	Harry, born January 10, 1874, is a Motorman, Springfield, Ills.
162.	iii.	Cora, born Feb. 12, 1879.
163.	iv.	Flora, born May 25, 1883.
164.	v.	Ira, born Feb. 20, 1887.

7J.   WILLIAM HENRY[5], (*Joshua*[4], *Peter*[3], *John*[2], *Christopher*[1]), born Feb. 1, 1845, married Oct. 17, 1866 to Ophilia J. Leighton, who was born Feb. 17, 1848. They now reside at No. 2310 Twenty-first Street, Omaha, Nebraska.   He was born in Topeka, Tazewell Co., Illinois and received a common school education.   At the age of nineteen years he enlisted May 2, 1864 in Co. C., 139 Illinois Infantry, and held the rank of Second Corporal for the term of 100 days, having been discharged Oct. 24, 1864.   In 1867 he formed a partnership with his father and continued business in that shape until the father's death in 1882.   Then his brother, Frank R., was substituted as a partner in his father's place.   The new firm continued in business until 1887, the partnership was dissolved by mutual consent and William Henry embarked in business alone.   In 1892, he removed to Peoria, Illinois, and in 1894 sold out and moved to Omaha, Nebraska. Here he formed a partnership with his two brothers-in-law in the Roofing and Pile Driving business.   The 139th Illinois Regiment, to which he belonged, was used for guard and provost duty in Illinois, Kentucky, Missouri and Tennessee.   Mr. Wagenseller has in his posession a certificate of thanks from the best President that ever lived.   It is a just pride with which he cherishes that document.   The Document reads as follows :

THE UNITED STATES VOLUNTEER SERVICE.

THE PRESIDENT'S THANKS AND CERTIFICATE OF HONORABLE SERVICE.

To Corporal William Henry Wagenseller,—

Whereas, the President of the United States has made the following executive order returning thanks to the Volunteers for One Hundred days from the States of Indiana, Illinois, Iowa and Wisconsin, to wit,

Executive Mansion,
Washington City, Oct. 1, 1864.

The term of One Hundred days for which Volunteers from the States of Indiana, Illinois, Iowa and Wisconsin, volunteered under the call of their respective Governors in the months of May and June to aid in the recent campaign of General Sherman having expired the President directs an official acknowledgment to be made of their patriotic service. It was their good fortune to render efficient service in the brilliant operations of the South-West and to contribute to the victories of the National Arms over the Rebel forces in Georgia under command of Johnson and Hood. On all occasions and in every service to which they were assigned their duty, as patriotic Volunters, was performed with alacrity and courage for which they are entitled to, and are hereby tendered the NATIONAL THANKS, through the Governors of their respective States. The Secretary of War is directed to transmit a copy of this order to the Governors of Indiana, Illinois, Iowa and Wisconsin and to cause a certificate of their honorable service to be delivered to the officers and soldiers of the States above named who recently served in the Military forces of the United States as Volunteers for One Hundred Days. Now, therefore, this certificate of Thanks and of Honorable Service is conferred on Corporal William Henry Wagenseller in token of his having honorably served as a volunteer for One Hundred days in C. Company, 139th Regiment Illinois Volunteer Infantry.

Given under my hand at the City of Washington this

15th day of December, in the year of our Lord one thousand eight hundred and sixty four.

By the President, ABRAHAM LINCOLN,
Edwin M. Stanton, President of the U. S.
Secretary of War.

William and Ophilia Wagenseller had five children as follows :

165.	i.	Fatina May, born Nov. 14, 1867, married May 22, 1889 to L. C. Loel of Pekin, Illinois. They have three children (1) Henry Wagenseller, born Dec. 22, 1890. (2) Anna Maude, born Sept. 2, 1893. (3) John Frederick. born March 22, 1896.
166.	ii.	Fannie M., born Jan. 7, 1871.
167.	iii.	Joshua Eugene, born Oct. 27, 1874. Afflicted with epileptic fits.
168.	iv.	William Henry, Jr., born May 26, 1878.
169.	v.	George Rupert, born Dec. 11, 1884.

76. FRANK RUPERT[5], (*Joshua*[4], *Peter*[3], *John*[2], *Christopher*[1]), born December 30, 1851, was married in Pekin, Illinois January 16, 1873 to Agnes Reynolds by Rev. S. D. Bell. Residence, 312 Buena Vista Avenue, Pekin, Ills. He is dealing in Dry Goods, Notions and Leather Goods at 302 Court Street. This union has been blessed with six children :

170.	i.	Jessie May, born Nov. 7, 1873. Married June 15, 1892 to Gus. Vincent Lincoln, of Peoria, Ills., now City Salesman for Robert Stevenson and Co., wholesale druggists of Chicago. Resides now at No. 250 East 60th Street, Chicago Illinois. No issue.
171.	ii.	Clara Daisy, born Nov. 8, 1875.

172.   iii.   Frederick Albert, born Dec. 5, 1877.
                     Is in business with his father.
173.   iv.   Frank Edward, born May 20, 1881.
174.   v.   Leroy Reynolds, born Sept. 11, 1885.
175.   vi.   Paul Weldon, born July 31, 1896.

All the children have been baptized in St. Paul's
Episcopal Church. The two daughters are confirmed
members of the same church.

77. WILLIAM JEREMIAH⁵, (*William Findley⁴*,
Peter³, John², Christopher¹), born March 23, 1839 and
died Aug. 3, 1895 in the borough of Selinsgrove, hence at
the time of his death he was 56 years, 4 months and 10
days old. Early in life he made his home with Henry
and Catherine Bickhart in Washington township, who later moved to Penns township near Kantz postoffice. His
education was obtained in the public schools. On November 5th, 1861, he was married to Rebecca Forry, daughter of John and Esther [Zerbe] Forry of Penn township.
His married life had not continued very long until the cri-
sis of the late Rebellion arose and the call to arms of able-
bodied men to defend the Union of this country brought
him to the front. On the 28th day of October 1862, he
entered the service of the United States as Corporal of Co.
F., 172nd Regiment of Pennsylvania Troops. His term
of enlistment expired and he was discharged Jan. 28, 1863.
He again enlisted and was assigned to Co. D., 208th Regiment, Pennsylvania Volunteers. He was mustered into
service Sept. 5, 1864 and was appointed to the position of
Sergeant of his Company. He was mustered out June 1,
1865 at the close of the war. His Commission as Sergeant was handed to him, Oct. 5, 1864, at Bermuda Hundred. He engaged in the fight at Fort Steadman and in
the capture of Petersburg, Va.

At the close of the war, he returned home and settled
down to pursue the life of a civilian and for several years
engaged in farming. In 1875 the Grange Movement became prevalent and June 18th, Penn Grange was organized
and Mr. Wagenseller became its first worshipful master.

W. J. WAGENSELLER.

1839-95.   [NO. 77.]

The Snyder County Pomona Grange was organized in 1881 and for several years he was the Presiding Officer of this body.

In 1883 the Grange idea of establishing co-operative stores became a reality and a place of business was opened in Selinsgrove. The corporation was known as " Farmers' Exchange, Limited" and W. J. Wagenseller was chosen as General Manager and Superintendent. This business was carried on until November 1890 when he voluntarily re-signed and retired to private life until his death. He never aspired to a political office though upon several occasions he was elected to fill positions in the district where he lived. He was a member of the Reformed Church at Selins-grove and an officer of the congregation. The widow and children as found below all reside at Selinsgrove, except George, who resides in Middleburgh and is editor and pub-lisher of the "Post." William J. was very methodical. He began to keep a diary when he first entered the service of Uncle Sam and he continued the keeping of it every day up to the time he took his bed with his final sickness. These daily records, now preserved, form a history of his daily life in minute detail and they contain many interest-ing notes of the people with whom he came in contact. Loyal to the duties of manhood he forged his way to the front as a living example of good citizenship and a worthy type of christian fortitude. By his sober, diligent and ag-gressive habits, he threw about himself the armor of a strong protection against the vices and snares of every-day life and clothed himself with that mantle of inspiration that draws to itself the exalted opinion of manly virtues. Wil-liam J. and Rebecca Forrer Wagenseller are the parents of ten children :

176.	i.	Kate Alice[6], born Feb. 22, 1862, is unmarried and a milliner at Se-linsgrove, Pa.
177.	ii.	Mary Louisa, born May 17, 1864 and died Aug. 25, 1865.
+178.	iii.	John Franklin, born Aug. 1, 1866.

+179.   iv.   George Washington, born April 27,
                       1868.
180.   v.   Infant son, born April 28, 1870
                       and died May 5, 1870.
181.   vi.   Ida May, born May 5, 1870.
182.   vii.   Amon Sylvester, born Nov. 11,
                       1873. Married August 8, 1897 to
                       Jeneatte Smith. They have a son,
                       Bruce Sylvester, born February 23,
                       1898. Residence, Selinsgrove, Pa.
183.   viii. Anna Celesta, born June 10, 1876
                       and died Feb. 17, 1882.
184.   ix.   Charles Henry, born Dec. 9, 1877
                       and died July 24, 1878.
185.   x.   Infant son, born Sept. 30, 1881 and
                       died same day.

78.   MARTIN LUTHER[5], (William Findley[4],
Peter[3], John[2], Christopher[1]), born Sept. 6, 1840, married
December 7, 1865 to Carrie L. Kistner, who was born
July 13, 1840. Residence, Selinsgrove, Pa. He received
his early education in the public schools, and when Missionary Institute (now Susquehanna University) was found-
ed he was enrolled as one of the first students. After completing two years, his health failed, and he was compelled
to cease his attendance at school. He, however, after that,
taught one year in one of the public schools of the county.
When the Civil War broke out, he left his occupation as a
clerk in a store, and enlisted as a private in Co. F., 131st
Regiment, Pa. Vol. Inf. and served with distinction, having
been mustered out as a Lieutenant of the Company. He
participated in the engagements of Antietam, Fredericksburg, and Chancellorsville, also on the raid known as
Burnside's Muddy March. Upon returning home again,
he entered a store as clerk. In 1866, he entered into partnership with his father in the mercantile business under
the firm name of Wagenseller & Son. His father died in
1876 and about a year thereafter, he closed out the business. In 1864 he was made a member of the Masonic

Lodge (Lafayette No. 194) of Selinsgrove, was its efficient Secretary for many years, also Treasurer, and filled the positions of Junior Warden, Senior Warden and Worshipful Master and also Representative to the Grand Lodge. In 1866 he passed through the Chapter, Council and was made a member of the Crusade Commandery, located at Bloomsburg, but from all of the above, he has resigned except the Lafayette Lodge. In February 1867 he became a charter member of the first Grand Army Post in Snyder County (No. 28) but owing to the carelessness of its officers the Post was finally disbanded. In 1880 he again became a member of the Grand Army in Capt. Davis Post, No. 148, located at Selinsgrove. He was Adjutant for a number of years, Officer of the Day, and Post Commander three years. It was often said of him that it was only through his work and influence that the Post was kept alive. He was repeatedly appointed on the Staff of the Department Commanders, also of the Commander-in-Chief of the United States and for three years in succession he was elected a member of Department Council of Administration, and also many times selected to inspect Posts and Districts. In early life he identified himself with Trinity Lutheran Church, and Sunday School as a scholar, teacher and Librarian. The latter position he held for over twenty-five years and still continues in the work. He was president of the County Sunday School Association for nine years in succession during which time the association meetings largely increased in interest and attendance. At the age of 16, he became a member of the Choir attached to the above named church and he still occupies a place there. In 1877 on account of the resignation of Mr. Geo. Schnure as a member of the Board of Directors of Missionary Institute (now Susquehanna University) and at the instance of Mr. Schnure our subject was elected to fill the unexpired term of Mr. Schnure. He has continued ever since to be a member of the Board, having been its efficient Secretary since 1887. While a student of the school he helped to organize the Philosophian Literary Society being for a long time its Secretary and he remained a true and staunch member for many years. Mr. Wagenseller has always been strongly attached to the Institution, and as a member of the Board has done much to gain for it, its present success. In all the time of his membership of the Board, he has very rarely missed a session. In politics he has always been an ardent Republican, working for the success of those principles. Was never an aspirant for political office, although many times solicited, he always refused. He has been an advocate of the temperance cause and now in his daily life is a living example of the principles he has espoused.

To M. L. and Carrie L. Wagenseller have been born five children :

186.	i.	Edgar Newton, born Mar. 6, 1869, and died Feb. 19, 1870.
187.	ii.	Luella May, born July 29, 1871, and died June 1, 1873.
+188.	iii.	Benjamin Meade, born June 22, 1873.
189.	iv.	Carrie Mabel, born Jan. 14, 1875 and died Sept. 2, 1894.
190.	v.	William Ralph, born Nov. 18, 1879.

83. SIMON CAMERON[5], *(John Neilor[4], William[3], John[2], Christopher[1])*, born Aug. 13, 1852, in Tamaqua, Pennsylvania. His father's family moved to Pekin, Ills., where they lived four years and then moved to Sing Sing, New York. In 1872, after his father's death, he went to Sunbury, Pa. to his Uncle George and secured employment with the Northern Central Railway Company. After ten years' service with the Railroad Company, he went into the mercantile business in Shamokin, Pa. and remained in it until 1894. He was then appointed as postmaster of Shamokin by President Benjamin Harrison and was commissioned to serve for four years, which he did very successfully. It was our subject who introduced the free delivery system in Shamokin during his term. He has held the position of Assistant Burgess of Shamokin. He is now

M. L. WAGENSELLER,

SELINSGROVE, PA. [NO. 78.]

in the insurance business having formed a partnership with Samuel Heckert. They are doing business under the name of Wagenseller and Heckert. On April 13, 1878 he married Laura M. Bittenbender.

S. C. and Laura are the parents of four children, as follows :

191.	i.	Walter B.[6], born Jan. 10, 1879 and and died April 8, 1880.
192.	ii.	Harriet S., born Feb. 26, 1882.
193.	iii.	Sarah McVeagh, born Feb. 5, 1884.
194.	iv.	Mary E., born March 30, 1887.

84. GEORGE[5], (*John Neilor*[4], *William*[3], *John*[2], *Christopher*[1]), was born August 28, 1862, at Sing Sing, N. Y. He received a common school education and attended the private school of Prof. Rambo at the Trappe, Montgomery County, Pa. for one year. On the sixth day of December 1881 he was apprenticed for four years to the Machinist trade at the Sunbury Shops of the Pennsylvania Railroad Company. He received his certificate as Machinist, December 6, 1885. On March 8, 1888, he was appointed Engine House Foreman at Nescopeck, N. and W. B. of the Penna. R. R. Co. He was married to Mary E. McClow who was born March 1864. They have a family of six children :

195.	i.	Simon Cameron[6], born Oct, 18, 1886.
196.	ii.	Laura, born March 20, 1888.
197.	iii.	George Oliver, born Oct. 7, 1889 and died April 20, 1896.
198.	iv.	James Kerchner, born Sept. 19, 1891.
199.	v.	Anna Marguerite, born Oct. 30, 1893.
200.	vi.	Mary Elizabeth, born Sept. 2, 1895.

86. MARTHA[5], (*David Schrack*[4], *Jacob*[3], *John*[2], *Christopher*[1]), born Jan. 14, 1836, married Sept. 11, 1853, in Philadelphia by Rev. M. G. Clark of the Temple Bap-

tist Church, to Seth Humphrys, a carpet and yarn manufacturer, born Dec. 25, 1827, resides at Gladwyne, Pa. They are the parents of seven children, (1) Seth G. Humphrys, born Sept. 27, 1854 and died Sept. 25, 1855. (2) Mary Ellen Humphreys, born April 10, 1856 and died June 12, 1868. (3) Anna M. Humphrys, born April 23, 1858, married January 2, 1875 to Alfred S. Heft. Anna died June 16, 1887. This union was blessed with three children, Seth, born Nov. 18, 1879, Bessie, born Sept. 1, 1881 and Jacob, who died in infancy. (4) Clara Maud Humphrys born May 21, 1860, married July 31, 1879 to Dr. Alfred Mellersh, who was born Sept. 7, 1847 and now resides on the Corner of Lyceum and Manayunk Avenues, Manayunk, Phila., Pa. They have five children : Martha, born Aug. 26, 1880 ; Anna, born June 10, 1885 ; Mary, born June 6, 1888 ; Alfred, born Jan. 2, 1890 ; Edith May, born Sept. 20, 1896. (5) Enos Humphrys, born Feb. 18, 1863, married Dec. 12, 1888 to May V. Towns, who was born Dec. 3, 1861. Residence, Narbeth, Montgomery County, Pa. They have two children, Seth, born Dec. 20, 1889 at Ardmore and Alfred, born April 25, 1894. (6) Seth I. Humphrys, born Nov. 2, 1869, and died Oct. 29, 1875. (7) Mary Bessex Humphrys, born April 25, 1872, married November 10, 1892 to Frank C. Marshall of Haverford, Pa. They have a daughter, Anna Maud, born Sept. 9, 1893. He holds a lucrative position with the Real Estate Trust Company, No. 1340 Chestnut Street, Phila.

87. MARY[5], (*David Schrack[4], Jacob[3], John[2], Christopher[1]*), born June 16, 1837, married May 8, 1857 to George Mallison. She died June 18, 1865 of a complication of diseases. They had six children : (1) James Mallison, born Dec. 12, 1858, unmarried, resides at Chester, Pa. (2) Harvey P. Mallison born Feb. 6, 1860, married to Katherine Grayham, June 27, 1888. Residence, Lansdowne, Pa. They have 5 children, Mary, born May 12, 1889 ; George, born Feb. 3, 1891 ; Catherine born November 1892; Harvey born March 1892

and died June 16, 1896 and Dorothy born January 1898. (3) Anna Mallison, born August 6, 1862, married June 28, 1894 to Adam Witteman. They have a son, George, born May 22, 1895. Residence, No. 419 North 33rd Street, Philadelphia. (4) George Mallison, born March 6, 1864 and died Aug. 12, 1888. (5) Josephine Mallison born April 24, 1866. (6) John Albert Mallison born May 9, 1869 married Aug. 5, 1890 to Rose Snyder. They have one child, Alva, born Jan. 19, 1892. Residence, Hinkley Avenue, Ridley Park, Pa.

88. MARGARET ANN⁵, (*David Schrack⁴, Jacob³, John², Christopher¹*), born Oct. 7 1840, married Jan. 31, 1862 to Samuel E. Happersett. Residence, No. 221 New Street, West Chester, Pa. They have six children, (1) S. Humphrey Happersett, born Dec. 6, 1862, married Sara Benly March 24, 1887, residence Uwchland, Pa. They have a family of five children. (2) John W. Happersett, born March 2, 1864, married March 1, 1893 to Rachael McClintock. Residence, Downingtown, Pa. (3) Rachael A. Happersett, born Dec. 26, 1866, married March 28, 1888 to S. Wesley Jones of Downingtown, Pa. (4) Louis W. Happersett born Nov. 5, 1869, married June 15, 1893 to Martha E. Griffith. Address, Downingtown, Pa. (5) David Warren Happersett, born Dec. 29, 1873, resides at West Chester, Pa., and Samuel E. Happersett, born Feb. 14, 1875, died March 4, 1881.

89. LEVI⁵, (*David Schrack⁴, Jacob³, John², Christopher¹*), born Oct. 14, 1842, married Alice Raney. Levi swallowed four false front teeth and died of starvation, after undergoing an unsuccessful operation. The widow resides at 3911 Melon Street, Philadelphia, Pa. They had two children :

201.   i.   Anna, married John Pavet with whom she had two daughters, Mabel and Florence.

202.   ii.   Wellington, resides with his mother.

91. HARRIET⁵, (*David Schrack⁴, Jacob³, John²,*

Christopher[1]), born April 2, 1846, married Harry Town-
send who resides at 26th and Poplar Streets, Philadelphia.
They are the parents of ten children: (1) John Town-
send, born March 8, 1864, married Aug. 15, 1888 to Car-
oline Byrne who died Aug. 17, 1895. Address, 26th and
Poplar Sts., Philadelphia. They have had two children,
James, born March 12, 1891 and Edith born June 11,
1894. (2) Ida Townsend, born Dec. 17, 1865, married
June 6, 1888 to William Ziegler, who resides at 31st and
York Sts., Philadelphia, Pa. They have four children,
Gertrude, Edna, William and Raymond. (3) Anna Townsend, born Feb. 8, 1868 married June 16, 1888 to Frank
Fritz, who now resides at No. 1263 North 26th Street, Phil-
delphia. They have two children, Viola and Frank. (4)
Sarah Townsend, born May 8, 1872 married Nov. 14,
1891 to Edward Brown who resides at No. 863 North
26th Street, Philadelphia, Pa. They have one child Ethel,
born Sept. 13, 1894. (5) Martha, born Nov. 6, 1874,
married Nov. 11, 1896 to Harry Didall, who now resides
at 1263 North 26th Street, Phila. (6) William, born
Feb. 10, 1870, married June 29, 1893 to Bessie Win-
nings. (7) Harry Townsend, born May 13, 1877. (8)
Seth Townsend, born May 30, 1880. (9) Harvey Townsend, born April 23, 1882. (10) Mary Townsend, born
Aug. 17, 1884.

93. JAMES[5], (*David Schrack*[4], *Jacob*[3], *John*[2], *Christopher*[1]), born Jan. 1, 1849, married March 20, 1883 to
Esther A. Moore, who died Nov. 9, 1896. Residence, Glen
Moore, Chester Co., Pa. He was born in East Brandywine township, Chester County, Pa., and moved to Wallace township in 1856, to Glen Moore in 1883 when he
was married, moved to Downingtown in 1885, where he
remained only one year, returning to Glen Moore in 1886
where he now resides. He is one of the few Wagenseller's
who has accumulated considerable property, having attained a commercial rating of $50,000. He owns considerable
property in Wallace, East and West Nantmeal and West
Vincient townships, three houses in Glen Moore, where he

lives. A large park was opened in Glen Moore on Arbor
Day in the Spring of 1898 and he generously contributed
the land for the entire park. Upon the occasion of the
formal opening, he was given a vote of thanks and three
ringing cheers for the magnanimous gift. He had been a
farmer, but he now lives retired. He has settled several
large estates and now has several to manage. He is the
guardian and trustee for several estates and returns more
money as state tax on interest bearing money than any one
person in Wallace township. He and his wife, Esther,
are the parents of two children :

    203.   i.   Margaret A., born Nov. 9, 1883.
    204.   ii.   David Earl, born Feb. 14, 1890.

    96.   JOHN[5], (*Levi[4], Jacob[3], John[2], Christopher[1]*), born
March 27, ——, twice married, first to Elizabeth V. Sirlee,
now deceased, and second to Mary C. Irwin. For many
years he kept a general store at Thorndale, Chester County, Pa., and contributed largely to the public spirit of the
village. The iron works of that place having been closed
and many people moved away as a consequence, he closed
his business there and in the Spring of 1898 moved to
Pottstown, Montgomery County. He is now manufacturing and selling some medicine. He is the father of 9 children, 3 with the first wife and 6 with the second wife, as
follows :

    First marriage.
    205   i.   Carrie[6], born 1867, now deceased.
+206.   ii.   Alvin Worthington, born March
                26, 1869.
    207.   iii.   Clement Levi, born 1871, now de-
                ceased.
    Second Marriage.
    208.   iv.   Harry Ellis.
    209.   v.   Frank.
    210.   vi.   John Edgar.
    211.   vii.   Anna.
    212.   viii.   Florence May.
    213.   ix.   Nellie Irwin.

114.   JAMES K.[6], (*Thomas Weidner*[5], *George*[4], *John*[3], *John*[2], *Christopher*[1]), born July 17, 1850, married Polly Ann McCarter, Aug. 17, 1876.   Residence, Birds, Lawrence County, Ills.   To them were born seven children :

214.	i.	James W.[7], born Dec. 21, 1877 and died Sept. 1, 1895.
215.	ii.	John W., born Dec. 26, 1879 and died April 25, 1881.
216.	iii.	Eliza J., born March 22, 1882, married May 22, 1896 to Sullivan W. Richards. To them, a son, Albert Clinton[8], was born May 28, 1897, a representative of the eighth generation.
217.	iv.	Bertha B., born June 1, 1884.
218.	v.	Albert H., born Dec. 17, 1886.
219.	vi.	Emma E., born Sept. 6, 1892, and died Sept. 27, 1892.
220.	vii.	Burnice E., born Sept. 22, 1893.

117.   THOMAS HARLAN[6], (*William*[5], *George*[4], *John*[3], *John*[2], *Christopher*[1]), born July 7, 1847, was never married, and was killed June 23, 1897 by a fall of earth in a gold mine at Rico, Dolores County, Colorado.   He was a member of Co. H., 135th Illinois Volunteers in the late war.   Captain T. H. Wagenseller, as he was called, was in partnership with W. W. Parshall in the gold mining business.   We quote the following from a local paper at Rico, Colorado :

" He served eighteen months in the Union army during the late war as a member of Co. H., 135th Illinois, and since that time he has taken a great interest in military affairs, and was captain of the Rico military company a number of years, and was a member of the staff of Governors Routt and McIntire, with the rank of colonel.

The past seventeen or eighteen years he spent in mining and prospecting in the San Juan country, a greater portion of this time being spent at Rico.   He had been very hopeful during the past few months, and was sure that his portion of the proceeds from the Enterprise lease would enable him to be independent for the remainder of his life.

Captain Wagenseller was a good friend and open enemy. He was at all times patriotic and chivalrous, and while he angered easily, he was quick to forgive.

During the few days just prior to his death he had commenced to make arrangements for his approaching marriage with Miss Flora Keltow, one of our most highly respected young ladies, who has the sympathy of the community in her bereavement. In addition to the loved one, Mr. Wagenseller left a father, brother and sister to mourn his untimely demise.

The funeral occurred from the People's Congregational Church under the auspice of the Improved Order of Red Men, of which order he was a member of good standing. The remains were laid to rest in the beautiful cemetery of Silver Crescent Lodge No. 40, I. O. O. F., the last sad rites being performed by the comrades of Hazen Post, No. 63, according to the ritual of the Grand Army of the Republic, the salute to the dead being fired by Sons of Veterans.

RESOLUTIONS OF RESPECT.

Resolutions of veterans of the war of the rebellion upon the death of our late comrade, Thomas H. Wagenseller.

Whereas, Death has again entered our midst and without warning taken from our midst late comrade, T. H. Wagenseller, thus thinning our ranks that cannot be filled, and recognizing in him a comrade of solidierly bearing and conduct, of patriotic and loyal principles, who fought a good fight and responded to the last bugle call; it is therefore

Resolved, that we extend to the relatives and bereaved ones that fraternal sympathy which comradeship during the severe test of fire in the time of war ripened in the hearts of all true soldiers."

COMMITTEE.

127. WILLIAM RILEY[6], (Amos[5], George[4], John[3], John[2], Christopher[1]), born Dec. 11, 1853 in Crawford Co., Illinois. He was married in Jacksboro, Jacks County, Texas by Judge Williams of Indiana, Nov. 12, 1879 to Rosa May Putnam who was born at Rochester, Fulton County, Indiana, April 21, 1864 and went to Texas in 1878. William R. was raised in Indiana and went to Texas in 1875. He is an expert Blacksmith and now resides at Pella, Wise County, Texas. They are the parents of seven children:

221.   i.   Dora Theresa[7], born April 9, 1881, married Jan. 3, 1897 to J. D. Kile, with whom she had a daughter, Sarah May[8], born Oct. 16, 1897, one of the few representatives of the eighth generation.

222.   ii.   Mary Malinda, born May 9, 1886.

223.   iii.   John Riley, born Jan. 23, 1889.

224.   iv.   Pearl Jone, born July 9, 1892 and died Jan. 21, 1893.

225.   v.   Amos Warren, born Jan. 16, 1893.

226.   vi.   Bertha May, born Sept. 25, 1894 and died July 4, 1895.

227.   vii.   Clata Leota, born Aug. 7, 1896.

149. FRANKLIN JACOB[6], (Peter Richter[5], Jacob[4], Peter[3], John[2], Christopher[1]), born Oct. 8, 1855, in Selinsgrove, married Dec. 17, 1878 by Rev. H. B. Belmer to Mary L. Keely, daughter of Z. S. Keely of Selinsgrove. His early days were spent in attending the public schools of his native place. When about twelve years of age, he entered Missionary Institute (now Susquehanna University) at Selinsgrove and pursued his studies continuously until the spring of 1876. He then entered the Medical department of the University of Pennsylvania at Philadelphia, graduating from that institution as a full-fledged doctor in 1878. In the spring of 1883, he was elected a member of the Town Council of Selinsgrove and has been re-elected continuously ever since. He is now the presiding officer

GEO. C. WAGENSELLER,
SELINSGROVE, PA.   [P. 116.]

of the Council. As a public officer he has made a brilliant record and has done much to improve the town. Shortly after his election as a member of the Town Council, that body determined to construct a system of water-works for the protection of the town against the ravages of fire and for the conveniences it would afford the citizens in the requirements of daily life. The young physician was thoroughly imbued with the idea that the town needed such improvements and vigorously advocated the introduction and construction of the plant. He has been a representative of the State Board of Health and as such has been a most vigilant officer in caring for evidences and extending precautions against the spread of any contagious or infectious diseases. During the Summer of 1897 the Penn Telephone Company was chartered by the Commonwealth of Pennsylvania and Dr. F. J. is a heavy stock-holder and a director in the corporation whose lines extend all over Snyder County and make connections with all important points in Union and Northumberland counties. In the introduction of the shoe factory just opened in Selinsgrove and the construction of the large new buildings for that purpose, he filled a most important position as a member of the building committee, giving to the new industry a great deal of time and money. He has always been identified with every progressive movement of his town or county during his day.

As a careful, conscientious practitioner and close medical student, he has no superior in Snyder County. Ever watchful of every change in his patient and a diligent regard for his on her welfare, he enjoys a large and lucrative practice in a community where the name, Wagenseller, has been continuously associated with the practice of medicine for three-quarters of a century.

The descendants are:

228.   i.   Harry Franklin[7], born January 12, 1880.
229.   ii. Florence Louisa, born April 16, 1881.

150. GEORGE C.[6], (*Peter Richter*[5], *Jacob*[4], *Peter*[3], *John*[2], *Christopher*[1]), born in Selinsgrove, June 30, 1857, married June 1, 1881 to Lula, eldest daughter of Franklin J. and Catherine Schoch of Selinsgrove. His early education was obtained in the public schools of his native town. Later he entered Missionary Institute (now Susquehanna University) and continued until he was eighteen years of age. Then he entered the drug store of his father, afterwards becoming its proprietor. He continued his services in the drug store until 1884. He still retained the drug store, but now he entered into partnership with his father-in-law, F. J. Schoch, in the business of Milling, dealing in Grain and Coal and continued in these business relations until 1894 when the partnership was dissolved. Mr. Schoch retired from the business and George became the sole proprietor of the business, which he is still successfully conducting at Selinsgrove. He is a prompt, careful and judicious business man carrying with him the esteem of all with whom he comes into contact. During this time he has not been without some recognition in public life. He has earned the title of being a shrewd politician, whose influence is always noted when the returns are counted. In the borough of Selinsgrove, he served two terms (6 years) as school director. He was then elected a member of the Town Council and after serving only one year, he resigned in 1880 to accept the position of County Treasurer of Snyder County, which he held until Jan. 1, 1893. In the spring of 1893 he was elected Chief Burgess of Selinsgrove and held the office for three years. In May 1898, he was recommended by Congressman Mahon to be the postmaster of Selinsgrove. He is yet a very young man and has a bright future before him. George and Lula have two children :

230.   i.   Frank Schoch, born July 14, 1883.
231.   ii. George Jacob, born Jan. 10, 1886.

178. JOHN FRANKLIN[6], (*William J.*[5], *William F.*[4], *Peter*[3], *John*[2], *Christopher*[1]), born Aug. 1, 1866, unmarried, educated in the public schools, Bloomsburg State Nor-

mal School and Missionary Institute (now Susquehanna University). The early inclination of his youth and manhood took him to teaching school and thus to impart to the rising generation the ingredients so essential to true manhood and the proper development of noble citizenship. He has taught both in Union and Snyder Counties. He lives with his mother at Selinsgrove.

179. GEORGE WASHINGTON[6], (*William Jeremiah*[5], *William Findley*[4], *Peter*[3], *John*[2], *Christopher*[1]), born in Penn township, Snyder County, Pa., April 27, 1868, married Miriam Orwig, daughter of Dr. John W. and Margaret [Zellers] Orwig of Middleburgh, Snyder County, Pa., Oct. 22, 1896. She is a descendant of Gotfried Orwig, a native of Germany, who emigrated to America in 1741 and whose lineage will receive consideration in another part of this book. The boyhood days of Geo. W. Wagenseller were spent upon his father's farm, much of his time being devoted to wholesome out-door work. In 1889 when he was fifteen years of age his father became the General Manager of the Granger's Store at Selinsgrove and for several years George clerked there during the summer months, while attending the public schools in the winter. In March 1887 he entered Missionary Institute, now Susquehanna University, at Selinsgrove, having secured the necessary funds for his tuition and books through the diligent and careful saving of many small sums. On June 6, 1889, he was graduated, and during the following summer he became the Principal of the public schools of Cowan, Union County, where he taught with marked success for one year graduating five students on May 15, 1890. In September, of the same year he matriculated as a student of Bucknell University, at Lewisburg, Penn., entering the junior class. His summer vacations were devoted to canvassing by which he earned money enough to pay the expenses of his entire course, and on June 22, 1892, he was graduated from the classical course with the degree of A.B. Three years later he was granted the degree of A. M. from his Alma Master.

During the summer of 1892 the Pennsylvania National Guards were called out to quell the riot at Homestead, Pa., and Mr. Wagenseller went with the Lewisburg Company, spending eighteen days on duty. In August, 1892, he accepted the position of Professor of English and Science in the Coatesville Academy, but in the following January, having learned that his salary was in jeopardy, he resigned. In April, 1893, he began work as Principal of the Teachers' Normal School at Kermoor, Clearfield County, Pa., the course being completed in June. During the following summer he was offered three positions within ten days, viz: The Presidency of Palatinate College, at Myerstown, Pa., the Assistant Principalship of the public schools at Clearfield, Pa., and the Principalship of the Bloomfield Academy at New Bloomfield, Perry County, Pa. He accepted the latter and held the position until the spring of 1894, when he resigned to engage in the Newspaper business, the one occupation, he so much adored above all others. On March 17, 1894, in partnership with A. E. Cooper, he purchased from Thomas H. Harter, *The Middleburgh Post* with the entire printing plant. This paper was originally established about 1844-5 in New Berlin, Union County, Pa., by Christian Moeser and was known as the *Union Demokrat*, a strong whig paper, published in the German language. In 1850 the *Demokrat* passed into the hands of Israel Gutelius. He continued its publication in New Berlin until 1853 when it was moved to Selinsgrove. It was continued as a German paper until 1861 when it was converted to an English paper and the name was changed to *The Post*. During the closing days of 1866, Jeremiah Crouse purchased the *Post* and moved it to Middleburg, beginning publication the first or second week in January, 1867. In December 1882, T. H. Harter became the owner and remained at the helm until March 17, 1894, when Wagenseller & Cooper purchased the plant as above recited. The partnership, thus formed, was short-lived for Dec. 12th, the same year, it was dissolved, Mr. Cooper retiring and Mr. Wagenseller became

the sole owner and has since ably conducted the enterprise alone.   Feb. 3, 1898, the plant was moved into a large two-story structure near the center of Middleburgh, erected especially for this printing plant.   It is in this building where the "History of the Wagenseller Family in America" first saw the light of day.   The *Post* is a strong Republican organ, free to expose wrong-doing in public life at any time.   It was through the industry and vigilance of our subject that the influence of the paper was greatly extended and he has added to the printing plant from time to time such modern devices as are required in an up-to-date office.   He is a member of Lafayette Lodge, No. 194, Free and Accepted Masons, located at Selinsgrove.

Early in 1896, learning that there never had been a united, determined effort made to gather the data concerning the Wagensellers in this country, and much less to have it published, he set to work to accomplish that result. He never realized what a massive and cumbersome task he had undertaken.   He had everything to learn and met many stumbling blocks, but an indomitable will surmounted all difficulties that were surmountable.   This volume is given as the result of his efforts ; where deficiencies occur, it is owing to inability to get replies to inquiries.   The extent of his success in this undertaking must be left to the reader.   Our subject resides at Middleburgh, the County Seat of Snyder County, Pa.

188.   BENJAMIN MEADE[6], (*Martin Luther*[5], *William Findley*[4], *Peter*[3], *John*[2], *Christopher*[1]), born June 22, 1873, educated in the public schools of Selinsgrove and Missionary Institute, having graduated from the latter institution in 1891.   Later he entered the Junior class at Bucknell University, Lewisburg, from which institution he has since graduated.   He taught one year as Assistant in the Academy at Rising Sun, Maryland and now holds an important position in the public schools of Milton, Pa.

206.   ALVIN WORTHINGTON[6], *John*[5], *Levi*[4], *Jacob*[3], *John*[2], *Christopher*[1]), born March 26, 1869.   His oc-

cupations have been various during the period of his manhood, having secured his first experience, that of general
clerk in his father's store at Thorndale, remaining with
him until he was 21 years of age, in the meantime having
attended their district public school, Downingtown High
School and one year at West Chester State Normal School,
He left his home as a Telegrapher with the Penna. Railroad,
remaining with that Company for two and one-half years
when his ambition to follow Horace Greely's advice set
his mind on seeing the West.   He resigned his position
with the Penna. R. R. and started for Denver ; soon after
arriving there he accepted a position of Asst. Agent with
the Union Pacific R. R. at Pine Grove, Colo., remaining at
that point just nine months, when he was transferred to a
similar position at Idaho Springs, Colo., on the Colordao
Central R. R., at which point he served both the Union
Pacific R. R. and later the U. P. D. & G. Railway. About
ten months after his arrival at Idaho Springs he was offered
a position in Reading, Pa. with S. M. Hess & Bro. as
book-keeper, etc. and accepted it.   He left this firm's employ in March 1895 having in the meantime accepted a
position in the office of the Southern Pacific Co. in Philadelphia.   In Nov. 1895 he went to the Philadelphia Bourse
as Assistant to the Secretary, leaving their employ in February 1898 to engage in his present work, that of Secretary to the General Passenger Agent of the Plant System
of Railways and Steamship lines at Savannah.   His address
is No. 311 Jones Street, Savannah, Ga.

[This completes the Main Genealogical Tree of Christopher Wagenseil.   The remainder of the book will be devoted to kindred branches of the family, sketches of persons
not herein given and Notes of interest to the Family.   Au-
THOR.]

Descendants of Catherine³ Wagensel= ler and Conrad King.

In compliance with the announcement made near the top of page 28 under the consideration of No. 6 in the family tree, we devote this chapter to the King branch of our family. With the greater portion of this branch there is a double relationship to the Wagensellers through the Evans family. This chapter is compiled almost entirely from information collected by Jesse Benner Evans of Uwchlan, Chester County, the husband of Sarah Susannah Wagenenseller (No. 55, Family tree.) Ezra Evans, the father of J. B. Evans, married Eliza King, a daughter of Conrad King and Catherine Wagenseller. Catherine was born Dec. 3, 1764 in Upper Hanover township, Philadelphia, now Montgomery County, Pa., was baptized at the New Hanover Church, April 7, 1765, by the pastor of that church. She married Conrad King, who is reported to have died in 1880 at the age of 80 years, hence born in 1800. This is certainly an error as they have children born prior to that time. Conrad and Catherine had nine children. We are not provided with the dates of birth, hence we can not insure a Chronological order. The children are as follows:

JOHN KING BRANCH.

I. JOHN KING. We have failed to receive a complete record of John King's family. He has a son, Conrad, still living at the age age of 83 years and a son Joseph G. residing at Uwchlan, Chester County, Pa., married to Mary Beaux. They have three children (1) Charles A.

King married to Alice Latshaw. He is living in Colorado and is divorced. They have three children. Names unknown. (2) Sarah King married George A. Wolff, a Methodist minister residing in Philadelphia. They have two children, Florence and Gertrude. (3) Frank P. King married Miss —— Beerbomer, now deceased. No issue. He was married the second time and has since been divorced.

II.   GEORGE KING, who died at the age of 20 years.

THE KEELY BRANCH.

III.   MARY KING, married to Mathias Keeley. To this union five children were born:

1.   John Keely, married to Mary Longenecker. They had six children: (1) Wm. P. Keely married to Annie M. Hazlet, now reside at Phoenixville, Pa. (2) Clarence H. Keely married Emma Snyder. They reside in Phoenixville with two children, Gordon and Thomas A. Keely. (3) Mary Ann Keely, married Cyrus Moser. They have an only child, a son, William Moser, married to Anna Brook, who reside at Birdsboro, Pa., and have a daughter Mary Moser. (4) Edward M. Keely married Mary Hazlet. They have 2 sons, Lincoln and Elmer, and reside in Philadelphia. (5) Stevena B. Keely married John Widroder. No children. Residence, West Philadelphia. (6) One of John and Mary Keely's children died in infancy.

2.   Joseph Keely, the second son of Mathias, married Anna Markle and died recently at Spring City, Pa. At the time of his death he was President of the National Bank of Royersford and also Burgess of Spring City. They had two children, (1) Oliver B. Keely married Mary Stauffer. Oliver and Mary had a daughter, Clara, now deceased. Mary resides at Phoenixville. He was successful foundryman and was killed in a railroad wreck at Spuyten Dyville in N. Y. He was a Past Master of Lodge, No. 453, F. and A. M. (2) Lovina Keely married to Enos Shantz. They are both dead, and an only son, Joseph K. Shantz, resides at Spring City, Pa.

MRS. CATHERINE K. PALMER. —TWINS— MRS. SARAH SCHOFIELD.

3. Catherine Keely married Joseph Kimes both of whom are dead. They had five children: (1) Josephine Kimes married Albert Hancock, now deceased, to whom were born Frank Hancock, a doctor of West Philadelphia and Catherine Hancock of the same place. (2) Eliza. (3) Catherine. (4) Emma Kimes. All unmarried. (5) Sarah Kimes, married first to William Cammel, now deceased, and second to William Brady, now deceased. A son, Harry Cammel, resides in Philadelphia.

4. Levi Keely moved to California soon after the discovery of gold and owned an extensive fruit farm. He married a woman out West with whom he had two children. All are dead.

5. Mary Ann Keely died at the age of 16 years.

THE DOLBY BRANCH.

IV. CATHERINE KING married Abram Dolby. They had eleven children:

1. Abel Evans Dolby of Vineland, N. J., born about 1815.

2. Newlin Dolby, married Sarah Allison, both dead.

3. Sarah Dolby, twin sister of Catherine, born April 6, 1817, married George Schofield, now deceased. They had two children: (1) Cecelia Jane, married William K. Hanson. Resides at Haddonfield, N. J. and has two unmarried daughters. (2) Ida Melvina, unmarried.

4. Catherine King Dolby, twin sister of Sarah, born April 6, 1817 in Uwchlan township, Chester County, Pa. Married Dec. 28, 1837 to Mifflin Leonard Palmer. He is a Morman Elder, a polygamist in belief, not in practice, feeling that one wife is enough. The Palmers now reside at 512 State Street, Salt Lake City, Utah. They had 8 children as follows: (1) Rebecca West Palmer, born Oct. 2, 1838, near the Eagle, in Uwchlan, Chester County, Pa. She was married Feb. 6, 1862 to Lewis A. Harper, who died August 4, 1889. They had six children, (a) Kate Palmer Harper born April 6, 1863 and died Nov. 13, 1867, (b) Sallie Harper born March 28, 1866, died April 18,

1866, (c) Ella Phoebe Harper, born Dec. 1, 1867, (d)
Charles Morris Harper, born Feb. 3, 1870, died May 27,
1873, (e) Benjamin Franklin Harper, born Sept. 28, 1874,
(f) Brinton Conrad Harper, born July 1, 1870 died May
1, 1882. These children were all born in Reading, Pa.
The widow and children now reside at 718 Chestnut St.,
Reading, Pa. (2) Phoebe Couch Palmer, born Jan. 9,
1840, near Eagle in Uwchlan, Chester Co., Pa., married
July 31, 1861 to John G. Schaffer, who died Dec. 31,
1889. No issue. Residence No. 511 State St., Salt Lake
City, Utah. (3) Selinda Dolby Palmer was born in
Brandywine township, Chester County, Pa., Jan. 31, 1842.
She was married Sept. 27, 1862 to William A. Bringhurst
of Salt Lake City, Utah. They had ten children, (a) Wm.
A. Bringhurst, Jr., born Sept. 29, 1863 in Salt Lake City,
married March 30, 1886 to Martha Granger. They have
six children: William Walter, born Dec. 25, 1886; Arch-
er, born April 23, 1888; Clara, born Nov. 16, 1889; Benjamin, born June 5, 1891; Selinda, born Feb. 5, 1893,
Laura, born Aug. 14, 1895. (b) Howard Bringhurst;
born Aug. 14, 1865 in Salt Lake City, was married to
Laura Davis to whom was born one child, Howard Leland
Bringhurst, April 10, 1897. (c) Eliza Buthula Bringhurst, born March 14, 1868 in Toquerville, Washington
County, Utah. She married Marion Kleinman with whom
she had four children : Howard Conrad, born Jan. 22,
1889 ; Mifflin, born November 8, 1892 ; Maroni, born
April 30, 1894 and George, born Aug. 4, 1896. Of the
four children, the first three were born in Toquerville,
Utah and the last at Oneida, Bannock County, Idaho. (d)
May Ellen Bringhurst, born February 3, 1870 in Toquerville, Utah, married to Walter Flack. They have three
children, all born in Toquerville, Utah : Selinda
born Jan. 12, 1891 ; James, born Feb. 19, 1893 and Walter H., Jr., born Oct. 23, 1895. (e) Mifflin Morris Bringhurst, born Feb. 26, 1872, (f) Lorenzo Bringhurst, born
March 13, 1874, (g) George R. Bringhurst, born March
3, 1876, (h) Franklin P. Bringhurst, born Jan. 19, 1878

in Toquerville, Utah, (i) Daniel Bringhurst, born Sept. 22, 1879, died April 8, 1882 and Henry Bringhurst, born Dec. 17, 1881, The entire family reside at Toquerville, Utah. (4) Eliza Evans Palmer, born Nov. 24, 1844 near Lionville, Uwchlan township, Chester County, Pa., married Nov. 2, 1867 to Edwin Frost. They have five children, (a) Edwin Palmer Frost, Jr., born April 7, 1870 at St. Thomas, Lincoln Co., Nevada, (b) Nettie Palmer Frost, born Mar. 5, 1874 in Salt Lake City, Utah, (c) Bessie Sula Frost, born Aug. 11, 1877, (d) Roy Palmer Frost, born Sept. 18, 1880, (e) Leo Palmer Frost, born Feb. 19, 1885. Residence, No. 337 Second East St., Salt Lake City, Utah. (5) Alphonso Morris Palmer, born Feb. 19, 1847 near Lionville, Chester Co., Pa., married Dec. 28, 1868 to Mary Frost. They had 12 children as follows : (a) Minnie Palmer, born in Idaho Nov. 5, 1870, married Oct. 16, 1889 to Harry W. Matthews. They had four children, Harry Harold, born Oct. 30, 1890 ; Clarence Elbert, born Dec. 31, 1892 ; Leo, born July 14, 1895, and Elmer, born Dec. 26, 1897. (b) May Catherine Palmer born Oct. 30, 1872, died May 8, 1884. (c) Zusetta Eliza Palmer, born Oct. 7, 1874, married Dec. 5, 1894 to Charles Cundich. They have two children, Charles Lester Cundich, born Nov. 25, 1895 and Mary Edith Cundich, born Sept. 26, 1897. Residence, Taylorsville, Utah. (d) Alphonso Morris Palmer, Jr,, born July 21, 1877. (e) Sarah Edna Palmer, born Oct. 29, 1879. Ruby Palmer, born Nov. 2, 1881. (f) Rufus Leonard Palmer born Sept. 15, 1883, (g) Bertie Conrad Palmer born Jan. 10, 1886. (h) Roswell Potter Palmer, born April 11, 1888. (i) Phoebe Effie Palmer, born Oct 17, 1890. (j) Mifflin Earl Palmer, born Oct. 5, 1892 and Abram Dolby Palmer, born Sept. 19, 1894. The birth places and places of residence of the above is Taylorsville, Salt Lake County, Utah. (6) Sarah Buthula Palmer was born at Loag's Corner, West Nantmeal township, Chester County, Pa., Jan. 30, 1851, married Feb. 12, 1872 to John C. Sharp. They have two children : (a) Joseph P. Sharp born at Vernon, Utah, Sept.

5, 1874 and (b) James Palmer Sharp born Aug. 17, 1877. Residence, Vernon, Utah. (7) Laura Irene Palmer, born Oct. 28, 1857 in Reading, Pa., died Oct. 2, 1858. (8) Esther Palmer, born July 17, 1860 in Reading and died July 21, 1860.

5. Eliza Evans Dolby married Abner J. Huzzard. Both are dead. They had five children : (1) Myra Gertrude Dolby married Wesley Engle to whom are born three children : (2) Catherine died at the age of 15. (3) Died in infancy. (4) Rudolph married Anna Dorlan. No issue. (5) Ella Marion, unmarried.

6. Selinda Dolby married Benjamin Jacobs, now deceased. They had four children : (1) Brinton Jacobs, married Kate Williamson and to them has been born one daughter. (2) Marry Emma Jacobs, unmarried. (3) Selinda Jacobs married Edward Humphrys. Two sons. (4) Laura Jacobs, now deceased.

7. Lewis Dolby, married Mary Dixey. They have three children, (1) Lansing Dolby, deceased. (2) Howard Dolby married and has two daughters, and (3) Lewis Fletcher Dolby, unmarried.

8. Thomas Dolby, died in infancy.

9. Melvina Dolby married Peter S. Davis. No offspring. Residence, No. 3934 Lancaster Ave., Phila.

10. Conrad King Dolby married Mary Lewis. They have a daughter, Ada. Residence, Morton, Delaware Co., Pa.

11. Emma Margaret Dolby (now deceased) married John Davis. They have one son, Geo. B. Davis, married to Augusta Copeland who also have a son. Mrs. Peter S. Davis and George B. Davis are in business at 3930-3936 Lancaster Ave., West Philadelphia.

PETER KING BRANCH.

V. ANNA MARGARET KING, married Peter King, (first cousin.) To them were born six children :

1. David King married Harriet Williams, residence, West Pikeland, Pa. They had one son, Peter, who married first Ellen May Gunkle, now deceased, and second

Martha King. Residence, West Pikeland, Pa. Peter and Ellen King have three children, Harry Clinton, Anna Betchtel and Hattie Williams King.

2. James King, died young.

3. Moses King, now deceased, married Matilda Lahr. They had eight children : (1) William Rufus King, now deceased, (2) Hannah Roberta King married R. Jones Patrick of West Chester, Pa. They have three children, Ambrose Park, Elwood Earl and Mary Elsie Patrick. (3) Smith Watkins King, now deceased. (4) Ambrose King, also deceased. (5) Sylvester King. (6) Theodore King. (7) Ida May King, now deceased, and (8) Leah Margaret King of West Chester, Pa.

4. Aaron King, now deceased, married Mary Trainor Mancill. Residence, Phoenixville. They had one daughter, Sallie Kate King, now dead, married to Frederick William Holmes with whom she had a son, Leon Edgar Holman.

5. Catherine Elizabeth King married Peter Wells. To them we credit three children : (1) Sallie Emerson Wells married to George Pennypacker of West Pikeland, Pa. (2) Daniel Edgar and (3) John Sherman Wells.

6. Jesse King, born March 1, 1829 married Sept. 7, 1854 to Lovina Miller, a daughter of John and Sarah Miller. Residence, Norristown, Pa. They had two children, Luther M., who died in infancy and Alonzo P. King, born July 26, 1865, married Kate Ryan, a daughter of P. and and Jenny Ryan. They reside at Norristown, Pa., and have five children in their family record : (1) Madaline King, born March 5, 1891, died June 5, 1897. (2) Jesse King born Feb. 19, 1892, died June 15, 1897. (3) Marion King, born Dec. 8, 1894. (4) Alonzo King, born Oct. 29, 1895, and (5) Jenny King born Feb. 6, 1897. Jesse King of Norristown, the grand-father of these, has devoted some time to Scientific pursuits. He has written up and published "The Mosaic Account of Creation," and has in manuscript form an "Elementary Work on Geology." ready to go to press as a text book to be taught in schools.

CONRAD SHEARER BRANCH.

VI. HANNAH KING married Conrad Shearer, both deceased. They had eight children:

1. Catherine K. Shearer, married first, Henry Fetters, second George Wiegand, all deceased. Two children with the first husband, Wm. Dallas and Isaac Fetters are dead. Four children were the fruit of the second marriage, (1) Ella C. and (2) H. Virginia Wiegand are unmarried and (3) E. Gertrude Wiegand married Samuel L. Watson who resides at No. 16 North 19th Street, Philadelphia. They have five children, Katie E., Samuel L., Ethel, Walter B. and George W. Watson. (4) John S. Wiegand married Alice Richardson. Residence, No. 16 North 19th Street, Philadelphia.

2. Elizabeth Shearer, married William Frederick, both deceased. They had two children, Ella Frederick, now dead, and Mary T. Frederick, married George O. Miller of Providence, R. I. They have two heirs, Harold and Florence Miller.

3. Dorothy Shearer, married William Strickland, both dead. They had four children, two daughters and Conrad are dead. Willamina, now dead, married Wilmer W. Baker. They had three children of whom Clara and Bessie Baker are dead and Edna resides with her parents on Berens St., West Philadelphia.

4. John B. Shearer married Mary J. Sherwood. Residence, Philadelphia. They are the parents of four children, Mary T. Shearer married to A. Eugene Pennewell, Antoinette S., now dead and Ara S. and Elmo Shearer.

5. Margaret K. Shearer, unmarried.

6. Mary Shearer, now dead, married Robert Todd. They had three children, a son Frank Todd, married Hannah Roth, Johanna Todd married Thomas Sharp and Annie Todd married to Howard Street. Thomas and Joanna Sharp have a son, Pearl.

7. Conrad Shearer married Alice Bockins. A child, name unknown, is dead. His whereabouts are unknown.

8. H. Rebecca Shearer married George Lambert.

EZRA EVANS BRANCH.

VII. ELIZA KING, born Dec. 6, 1799 married May 23, 1823, to Ezra Evans who was born Dec. 27, 1788 and died May 13, 1874. Eliza died Dec. 31, 1885. They had two children.

1. Newton Evans, born March 2, 1823, died July 14, 1897, married Hannah Acker, who was born Jan. 23, 1824. They are the parents of seven children : (1) Mary A. Evans married William D. Stitiler who have three children, Carrie, Penniah and Anna Stitiler. Residence, Chester Springs, Pa. (2) Ezra Evans, now deceased. (3) Isaac Evans, married Mary Ellen Smedley, to whom are born Clayton, Alice, Newton and Hannah Jane Evans. Residence, Mathews, Pa. (4) Acker Evans of Uwchlan, Pa. (5) William D. Evans, M. D., married Ada Moore. No issue. Residence, Philadelphia. (6) George W. Evans, Ticket Agent, Angora, Pa., and (7) Carrie Evans who died in infancy.

2. Jesse Benner Evans of Uwchlan, Pa., born Oct. 3, 1824 married July 15, 1851 to Sarah Susanna Wagenseller, born Dec. 15, 1831, the daughter of Dr. Jacob Wagenseller, late of Selinsgrove, Pa. For full list of children, see No. 55, page 71.

WILLIAM MOSES BRANCH.

VIII. HARRIET KING married William Moses who was born Sept. 4. 1804 and died May 12, 1893. Harriet King Moses was born June 14, 1803 and died April 8, 1891. Seven children were born to them.

1. Geo. D. Moses, born May 11, 1827, married first, Susan N. McWilliams, who died March 14, 1850. He married, second, Mary Tatem. Residence, 40th and Westminister Ave., West Philadelphia. Seven children are credited to the union with his first wife: (1) Robert M. Moses married Mar. 25, 1874 to Hannah Clerenstine. They had

seven children, Mary S., dead, George H., William L., Harford C., Robert H., Frederick E. and Ernest C. Moses. (2) Henrietta E. Moses, married Nov. 9, 1874 to Emanuel E. Ellwanger of West Philadelphia. They have two children, George D. and Susan Moses Ellwanger. (3) William N. Moses married May 1879 to Sarah Greeves. Residence, West Philadelphia. To them are born five offspring: Robert N., Ralph Greeves, Edward L., Helen and William Moses, the last mentioned being dead. (4) Amelia V. Moses married to William Walls to whom is born a son, Clarence W. Walls. (5) George C. Moses, dead. (6) John O. E. Moses, dead, and (7) Margaret S. Moses married to Charles R. Kentzler. No issue.

2. Newlin D. Moses, born Feb. 8, 1830, Residence, Merlin, Pa.

3. James L. Moses, born Sept. 27, 1832, married Julia Martin. They have one daughter, Ella May Moses who is married to Frank Happersett Wells.

4. Henrietta Moses, born Nov. 19, 1833.

5. William E. Moses born Dec. 14, 1837, married to Lizzie Mahan Dec. 25, 1873. They have two children, Edgar and Horace R. Moses.

6. Anna Lizzie Moses, born Dec. 23, 1841, died Dec. 26, 1842.

7. Anna Margaret King Moses, born Nov. 26, 1843, died June 3, 1858.

IX. REBECCA KING married John West.

Peter Wagenseller's Letter.

From Peter Wagenseller to his brother, William, describing the former's journey from Chester County, Pa., to Columbus, O., in the spring of 1834, just a year before Peter died. The letter is written in a neat clear hand on a large double sheet of paper. No envelope or postage was used, but the letter bears the Columbus, O., dating stamp, May 22 and "25" which doubtless represents 25 cents postage. The letter is as follows :

COLUMBUS, May 24, 1834.

DEAR BROTHER,—You must excuse me for not writing sooner. My head and my hand were so out of order from traveling that I could not compose myself to write until this day. Now I am going to give you an account of our journey. In the first place, we started on Thursday, April 17, and went as far as Peter Longaker's. Mother and Mary Ann were not well and we stopped there until Monday, the 21st, when we started and went to 3 miles above Reading, thence to Harrisburg, Carlisle, Shippensburg, Chambersburg, Bloody Run, Bedford, Son erset, Mt. Pleasant, and Robbstown on the Youghiougheny, a stream not as large as the Schuylkill, and thence on to the Monongahela river, where we crossed in a flat. They generally cross in a horse boat, but owing to the low water, the horse boat did not run. This stream is twice as large as the Schuylkill. Williamsport is on the bank of the Monongahela. Then we went to Washington and Alexandria on the Virginia line, then to Wheeling on the Ohio river. There are a great many smaller towns between the places mentioned.   I will now explain the road and the principal towns of the state of Ohio through which we passed.   Canton is on the Ohio river, opposite Wheeling. At this point the Ohio river is large.   We crossed it in a flat that runs over of itself in a very short time.   We next passed through St. Clairsville, Morristown, Fairview, Frankfort, Washington, Cambria, Zanesville, then crossed the Muskingon on a brigde.   The bridge forks in the mid-dle, the one bridge comes out above Licking Creek and the other below Licking Creek.   From Zanesville we traveled on the National Road to Akron and Columbus, having arrived in this city on Saturday, the 10th day of May, about 5 o'clock in the afternoon.   We were then all here except John and his family and mother.   Mary Ann was somewhat unwell and they remained back one day.   They arrived here Sunday afternoon all in good health and spirits.   Upon our arrival we drove up to a tavern kept by David Brooks, where we remained until Monday afternoon.   We then moved into two small houses and that is where we are now.   We have been looking around for farm land.   There is some land 5 or 6 miles from Columbus offered at $8 to $25 per acre.   [Here the writer describes some farms and gives prices which he and Matthew Chain examined with a view to purchasing.]   The situation of this town is on high ground, the main street running North and South on the Sciota river, the ground descending gradually both ways.   The city is large with a great many excellent brick buildings.   There are about 40 stone taverns.   The water here is rather hard on account of its being limestone water.   I would rather live on a farm than in town altogether among strangers; you feel somewhat lonesome.   There is a market twice a week and you can get anything you want.

Now I must tell you of the troubles we have had since we came to this place.   We moved on the 12th day of May to our present homes.   John and we live in two se-parate houses on the same lot and Matthew Chain and Hornetters live two squares away in one house.   On Sat-

urday, the 17th, toward evening Mary Ann took sick and
on Monday morning, the 19th, at 4 o'clock, a young
daughter was born. Mary Ann appeared to be as well as
could be expected. When she was in bed about an hour,
she began to complain of having pain. The doctor was
again sent for and everything possible was done to relieve
her, but all in vain. At seven o'clock the same morning,
she was a lifeless corpse. The spirit had fled and nothing
was left but a lump of clay. We hope she is resting
with Jesus where trouble shall cease and harmony
abound. She said when confined that she was not long
for this world; for what reason, she did not say. May the
Lord have mercy upon us and God grant we may meet
together in that world above where there is no mourning,
nor weeping, but singing praises to the Lord forever and ever.
On Tuesday, the 20th, ten o'clock was the hour appointed for the funeral, at which time the mother was laid in
the coffin and her daughter in her arms. A minister by
the name of Mr. Hough addressed the audience. His
text was taken from I Samuel, 3:18, "It is the Lord, let
him do what seemeth him good." There is a large scope
of country between us now and between Rebecca and
Susanna, our wives. Our lives are at God's disposal; our
time is in his hands and if we never see each other in this
world, may it please God to unite us again in the world
above where Jesus reigns foerever and ever. We are all
well and trying to get the thing most needful for our
souls.   I am your most aff. brother,
                                     PETER WAGENSELLER.
To William Wagenseller.

The original copy of the above letter is in the possession of Margaret Young, the youngest child of Wm. and
Rebecca Wagenseller. She is still living and resides at
Anselma, Chester Co. She is the oldest female descendant of Christopher Wagenseil living and is the last and
only living representative of the fourth genereation in this
country.

Susanna Longaker Wagenseller's Letter.

Through the courtesy of Mrs. M. E. Gearhart of Bloomsburg, we are permitted to publish the following letter written at the age of 81 years, only a few weeks before Susanna died. The letter is written in a clear, neat and steady hand and is addressed to Mrs. Gearhart, her granddaughter, as follows:

PEKIN, ILLINOIS, Feb. 19, 1862.

MY DEAR DAUGHTER,—I received your letter to-day and was glad to hear from you. You forgot to tell me whether your baby was a son or a daughter. I am glad to hear that all the folks are well and that Eddy can read in the Bible. My health is poor, I am very feeble at present and have not been to church all this winter. My lungs are affected and I feel as if I would drop off at any time. Our family are all well except myself. We have a nice daughter two months old. We call it Harriet M. Wagseller. I feel satisfied and happy, more satisfied and happy since we have had these protracted meetings than before. The meetings have continued for about six weeks and they have had a great many conversions. We have an excellent minister, Rev. Mr. Williamson. Salvation has come to our house and I feel very much rejoiced. I felt as if I ought to get up and make a noise too. Joshua Wagenseller has experienced religion. He told me that the Holy Spirit had been striving with him for about three years, but he thought he would resist it, but could not on

Sunday night four weeks ago. After they had all gone up stairs to go to bed, he told Harriet [his wife] that they ought to have family worship. She said they ought to have had it long ago and he came down and had prayer and now we have family worship every morning and evening and ask a blessing at the table. Religion has wrought a great change in this household. The next day he went to Hanover, and before he came home, he went to the store and and had a talk with Reuben and Lot and he said they all three cried like children. When he came home, he entered my room and told me all about it. He cried aloud. I thought then that my prayers had been answered. William Chain's wife has also been converted. I feel contented and happy, much more contented since Joshua has become a child of God than I did before. I hope he will hold out faithfully by the grace of God till death comes. I hope to make my way to Heaven and I will try to do His will.

We have a young men's prayer meeting every Sunday afternoon and a union prayer meeting every Friday evening. Joshua attends all of them and seems to be so earnest about going to church. My health is very poor. Some days I feel pretty well and others I can scarcely move about. My appetite is very good, but I have no strength, I am very weak all of the time. I have the consumption and am somewhat dropsical. I am in my 82nd year.

You wished to know about all the friends. Catherine and Timbrel were here to-day. They are well. Catherine's health is not very good, but it is better than it was some two years ago. I suppose you have heard Benny Timbrel was dead. He went to war and had——
[Here the letter must close as the last sheet has been lost or mislaid.]

By Way of Explanation.

We should state that Susanna, Peter's widow, was living with her son, Joshua, at the time the above letter

was written. The letter was probably written by some
one for her, as she grew up in a German neighborhood
and was compelled to take her education in German or
have none. She learned to read English from her children when they learned to read. She was a good reader,
a very bright intelligent woman for her day and very
companionable and industrious. The "Eddy" spoken of
in the letter was Mrs. Gearhart's oldest son, who was then
five years old. He read at four. He is preaching again,
but he is not in regular work. Preaching has been his
life work so far and will probably continue to be.
"Benny Timbrel" spoken of is the son of Catherine Wagenseller Chain Timbrel, (see page 50). "William Chain's
wife" is the wife of Catherine's eldest son. Her name is
Lou.

Susanna, the writer of the above letter, is described as
having a fair complexion with bright blue eyes, gray or
white hair.

The paper upon which the letter is written bears a
beautiful national emblem consisting of two right hands
clasped across a scroll of paper representing the Constitution of the United States, over which floats in brilliant
array the Stars and Stripes. Beneath the scroll is represented a tomahawk and other implements of warfare used
during the colonial period. It was just such a design as
Joshua would be likely to use during a period of civil
strife.

Jesse King's Letter.

NORRISTOWN, PA., May 2, 1898.

GEO. W. WAGENSELLER, A. M.,

MY DEAR SIR:—I received a communication from you a few days ago, which gave me great pleasure to receive. Some three months ago my niece, Mrs. Geo. Pennypacker, wrote to me for a genealogical record of my family, stating that a friend wanted the information. Who that friend was, I knew not; neither was it important I should know. I gave her a synopsis of it and thought no farther about it. Although I consider myself but an unimportant atom of the Wagenseller aggregation, still it affords me pleasure to think that I am yet remembered with those who gave me existence in this troublesome world. My grand-mother, Wagenseller, who was the mother of my mother, I do not remember. I remember my grand-father, Conrad King, and always will recollect riding with my uncle, Geo. Orner, (who had married my father's sister), in his "gig" in the train of my grand-father, Conrad King's funeral.

The second wife of Conrad King, my mother's step-mother, I well recollect. Her maiden name, I think, was Baugh, but Catherine Wagenseller, grand-father's first wife, I do not recollect.

My mother often spoke of her mother getting violent spells of cholic, which were periodical with her, when she or her sisters would hasten over the fields to a neighbor by the name of "Still" so that Mrs. Still would come to grand-mother's aid.

I well remember Wm. Wagenseller, brother to grand-
mother King, who was an uncle to mother. He and his
wife, Rebecca Wagenseller, often visited my father's home,
that was Peter King's near Pikeland churches.

I well remember the political meeting at Chester
Springs, when David R. Porter was running for Governor,
when James Wagenseller with others were firing an old
cannon called the "Diana," when, by a premature discharge, Mr. Wagenseller had his arm shot off. He was
the eldest son of three, James, George and John, who with
Ann Holman and Mrs. John Young formed the family of
Wm. and Rebecca Wagenseller.

I was not aware who our pioneer was. Do I under-
stand you to say it was "Christopher Wagenseil"? There
is no doubt it was.

Who was Geo. Wagenseller designated "of the
Wabash"? I knew Geo. Wagenseller, son of Wm. Wagenseller, who identified himself in politics to some extent,
as a protege of Simon Cameron. Or it was current political gossip at that day that he had the favor of Simon
Cameron who was often quoted as the "winebago chief"
by his opponents. I was but a boy and knew nothing of
their political differences, only from erratic conversation
among politicians of that day.

I have studied the science of Geology in the fields
from nature and have written it exactly in harmony with
Genesis, which will be a valuable adjunct to the Holy
Scriptures.

On the 21st day of September 1893, I went to a field
near the outer edge of our borough and there discovered
crystalized Indian corn which had evidently been planted,
cultivated and husked by the Antediluvian race. On a
subsequent visit to the same field I obtained a specimen
rock with a corn cob in it, projecting about ⅔ of an inch
above the surface of the rock, all bearing evidence of having been husked and piled on heaps ready to haul home

when the dread cataclysm came, which was November 17th, 1656 years after the creation.

I am glad to know that there has been energy enough found in one of our family to write up a work as important as the one you are engaged on. Very truly yours,
JESSE KING.

Life of Joshua Wagenseller,

WHICH WAS WRITTEN BY W. R. BRINK IN 1873.

"Joshua Wagenseller was a native of Montgomery County, Pennsylvania, born July 5th, 1813. He was the fifth child of Peter and Susanna (Longaker) Wagenseller. Mr. Wagenseller, father of Joshua, was a native of Montgomery County, Pa., and his parents were of German descent. He followed farming as the vocation of his life. He emigrated to Ohio about the year 1834 and settled in Columbus, Franklin County, where he resided until his death, which occurred about one year after. His wife, mother of Joshua, subsequently removed to Pekin, Ills., terminating a useful life in 1862, while residing with her son, Joshua. Mr. Wagenseller was a man who, by the even tenor of his disposition, had many friends; by his industry he provided well for his family and by precept and example exerted an influence over those committed to his care, which exerted a wholesome influence over his children and prepared them to become, by their industry and intelligence, useful citizens and prominent business men. He left the beautiful and picturesque scenery of of his native country and for the benefit of his family he followed the march of empire Westward, whereafter a limited sojourn in his western home—barely one year—he was taken from the embrace of the tender objects of his affection and called to try the realties of the future state.

The subject of this biography acquired his early culture mostly at Green Tree Seminary, in his native county when he acquired a knowledge of the rudiments of a good, practical business education. His first business engagement after completing this course was in a wholesale dry goods house in the city of Philadelphia, where he obtained a position as book-keeper and accountant. The next business engagemet was with his brother in Union county, Pa., where he remained about two years. Here he became familiar with the retail dry goods trade. We would remark that these experiences of his early life laid the foundation for that successful business career which in after life distinguished him in his subsequent mercantile transactions. He was now of age, and, looking westward for a richer field in which to engage, he went to Columbus, Ohio, and erected a saw mill on Elm Creek, and was engaged in the manufacture of lumber about three years, or until the Spring of 1837, when he removed to Illinois and settled in Pekin, Tazwell County. Mr. Wagenseller formed a partnership with his brother, Benjamin, and under the firm name of B. & J. Wagenseller. He began in Pekin, a course of mercantile life, which business he has since followed. This original firm ceased in 1844, by the death of his brother. They went through the financial crash of 1840 unscathed. This firm did not represent, at this time, a large financial capital, but were rich in muscle and energy, and by dint of that industry which knows no failure, they stood on a firm basis. Since the dissolution of this firm, Mr. Wagenseller has been at the head of subsequent business houses, and although he has been identified with other businesses largely in life, merchandising has been his leading vocation. He has been engaged in milling, covering an aggregate of nearly ten years. He rebuilt and owned the first good grist mill propelled by water in Tazwell county. Mr. Wagenseller began life on his own account with small financial means, and his subsequent success is the result of that combination of native powers coupled with his experience. He early learned the value and necessity of economy and industry in the accumulation of wealth. By his energy and correct judgment, he has gradually advanced financially until he takes a place among the opulent business men of Tazwell County. We mention this fact simply to illustrate what can be achieved by a proper energy when backed up with good business qualifications.

Mr. Wagenseller was married May 7, 1840, to Miss Harriet, daughter of Henry and Naomi Rupert, of Pekin, formerly of Virginia. As the fruits of this union, they had a family of six children. Mr. Wagenseller and wife are both members of the Congregational Church of Pekin, and are among the original members of that church. Mr. Wagenseller, in addition to his mercantile business, owns and carries on a farm near Pekin. He also owns a large area of land located in Iowa. He has been successful as a speculator in real estate, and has exhibited good judgment and skill in management and conducting of his large and varied business operations. Politically in early life, Mr. Wagenseller became a whig. His first vote for President was cast for Gen. William H. Harrison, in 1836. He was anti-slavery in his sentiments, and the following circumstance, as related by himself, opened his eyes to the inhumanity of the slave traffic. While on a trip to New Orleans, on a steamboat, a slave owner came on board with a woman and six children. He witnessed the revolting spectacle of a slave girl sold on the block. "That scene," said Mr. Wagenseller, "made me ever afterward an abolitionist." On the disorganization of the whig party, to which he has since been strongly attached, he voted twice for the Immortal Lincoln and twice for the vigilant Grant. He was acquainted with Mr. Lincoln and with his policy he cheerfully acquiesced. He was a firm supporter of the Union cause in this portion of state and was not of that number who faltered when the nation's life was in peril. Mr. Wagenseller has been required to represent the interest of his ward for several years in the common council of the city, and was vice president of Peoria, Pekin and Jacksonville Railroad Company. He has been one of the active, public-spirited citizens of Pekin for thirty-six years. Here briefly review the life of this venerable citizen, we find in his history the portraiture of a man who has, by his own energy risen step by step to a position of wealth and importance among the citizens of Tazwell county. His career has been marked by a good combination of business talent and moral rectitude which has given him an appropriate place in the affections and estimation of a large circle of acquaintances. He is appreciated for what he truly is, in the fullest sense of the sentence, a self-made man, with whom industry, self-reliance and business have become habitual. As a husband and parent, he is kind and affectionate. He has virtues peculiarly his own. His conceptions are not brilliant, but substantial. He is not imaginary, but real. His candor is embellished with honor; his acts are more the result of methodical thought than of impulse. Such is a brief view of some of the traits which make up the character of Joshua Wagenseller, who is a successful business man, needs no eulogy, as the record of an active upright life, for nearly forty years, leaves a more faithful record in the minds of his numerous acquaintances than it would be able for us to portray in the brief lines of his sketch." Joshua Wagenseller died on July 21, 1882.

From another source we get the following : Joshua Wagenseller was Treasurer of the Illinois River Railway for a term of four years, also was Treasurer of the Pekin Mechanical and Fair Association for three years. He was a very warm friend of Abraham Lincoln, and on account of Joshua's good business qualifications and mature judgment, President Lincoln tendered to Mr. Wagenseller, a cabinet position. Owing to Joshua's extensive business interests and possessing such strong domestic ties, he declined the magnanimous offer of the immortal Abraham. While forming his Cabinet, President Lincoln frequently consulted with Joshua and it was through the latter's recommendations, largely, that Hon. Simon Cameron was appointed to a position in Mr. Lincoln's Cabinet. During the war he gave a great deal of time and money to help the soldiers in the field.

It was through his influence that the citizens of Pekin organized and carried to successful completion a Sanitary Fair for the relief and benefit of Illinois soldiers. Nearly $3000.00 was raised in a week. Joshua was one of the original abolitionists of the West and was a staunch Republican all his life. In his early life in Illinois, he was interested in the under-ground railway, so called on account of assisting fleeing slaves through the country to freedom (Canada.)

He passed away in a ripe old age, after a long, active and useful life, having long held a leading position in local, business, political and social life. His memory is cherished by many besides his immediate relatives to whom his clear, practical good sense, seasoned by kindly feeling for the young and enterprising just entering the active scenes of business life; he manifested character by acts and words of more value to them as capital than silver and gold. His body and that of his wife lie buried in Lakeside Cemetery at Pekin, Illinois.

Theodore L. Wagenseller.

Theodore L. Wagenseller, who resides at No. 645
Everett Avenue, Kansas City, Kansas, (No. 72, page 84),
is the only child of Benjamin Wagenseller. Benjamin and
his brother, Joshua, moved to Pekin, Tazwell County,
Illinois, in the year 1836 and opened a store of general
merchandise. The firm did business under the name of B.
and J. Wagenseller until the death of Benjamin, March
15, 1844, when Joshua became the successor and sole proprietor of the business. Young Theodore lived with his
mother during his childhood years. His mother married
again and the family moved to Montrose, Iowa, opposite
Nauvoo, Illinois, a Mormon town. At Nauvoo is the
birth-place of Mormonism. It was at this place that Joseph
Smith, the Mormon leader, attempted to delude his fol-
lowers. He had some heavy planks placed out in the
Mississippi river about six inches below the water's surface, so as not to be visible to the naked eye. He was
going to prove to the people that he was the second Christ
and could walk upon the water. Either incidentally or
accidentally a section of his plank walk was washed out.
When Joseph Smith was walking upon the concealed
plank walk, his eyes turned toward Heaven and offering
up his devotions to Lord Jesus Christ, he suddenly dropp-
ed to the bottom of the river. Not being a swimmer, he
would have been drowned, had not some of his friends
come to his rescue. He afterward apologized to the congregation for the accident.

Leaving Montrose, Iowa, the suburbs of this Mormon

settlement, the family moved to Keokuk and then to Des Moines, Iowa. It is now the capital, but then it was nothing but a "wild and wooly" country. It was the headquarters for an Indian agency and several tribes came in every year to receive their annuities. The pay was red blankets, beads, and all sorts of trinkets. The family was located on a farm at Laconia about 30 miles south of Des Moines. For Theodore it was life in real earnest. During the Spring, Summer and Autumn it was all farm life. No church was nearer than eight or ten miles. Late in November a s chool was opened in a small log building, four miles distant. Theodore went to this school every day, rain or shine, reporting at nine o'clock in the morning and returning at four o'clock in the afternoon. Sometimes the snow would be three feet deep. The last week in January the school usually closed. While attending school, he was required to arise at four o'clock in the morning and it would be seven before he could complete all his chores. His mother being anxious to give her son a better education, she sent young Theodore to Chicago, where he devoted a full school year to hard study. While in Chicago, he lived with his grandfather, Lawrence Doyle. Leaving Chicago, he returned to Pekin to live with his uncle Jeshua, attending school and working in a store, morning and evening.

When the war broke out he enlisted in Company E., 47th Illinois Infantry Volunteers, Aug. 16, 1861 and the regiment was immediately ordered to Benton Barracks, St Louis, Mo. and afterward to Jefferson City, Mo., where they spent the winter. In the spring they were moved to Boonville, Mo., where they embarked on transports for Cairo, Illinois. Their regiment was then brigaded with the Fifth Minnesota, the Eighth Wisconsin, the Eleventh Missouri and Forty-seventh Illinois Inf. Vols. commanded by Major-General Joseph A. Mower. The Eighth Wisconsin was presented with a young American Eagle, which was with them in every battle in which they were engaged. Theodore was in the following named battles :

JOHN J. WAGENSELLER,
BLOOMSBURG, PA.   [P. 148.]

1. New Madrid, Mo., March 20, 1862.
2. Island No. 10, March 22, 1862.
3. Farmington, Miss., May 22, 1862.
4. Cornith, Miss, May 28-29, 1862.
5. Iuka, Miss., Sept. 19, 1862.
6. Cornith, Oct. 3-4, 1862.
7. Jackson, Miss, May 14, 1863.
8. Canton, Miss, May 20, 1863.
9. Assault on Vicksburg, Miss, May 22, 1863.
10. Siege of Vicksburg, Miss., which surrendered July 4, 1863 to Gen. U. S. Grant.
11. Fort De Russey, La., April 18, 1864.
12. The Red River Expedition under Gen. Banks.
13. Tupilo, Miss, July 14-15, 1864.

This is a good war record. He was mustered out of service October 11, 1864 at Springfield, Illinois.

Returning to Pekin, Illinois, he clerked in a dry goods store until the spring of 1866 when he went farther west and was engaged in making the preliminary survey for the Fort Scott and Memphis Railroad. In 1866 he was married and located permanently in Wyandotte City, Kansas, now changed to Kansas City, Kansas. Here he was agent for the United States Express Company for a number of years and afterward was appointed agent in Kansas City, Missouri, which position he held for a number of years. In 1883 he became a traveling salesman for the purpose of selling lumber, which occupation he follows more or less at the present time, affording ample opportunity for recreation.

In politics, he has always been a Republican, casting his first vote for Abraham Lincoln. Ever since, upon National questions, he has voted in harmony with Republican principles, and has never had occasion to regret his choice. With such satisfactory results in the past, he proposes to espouse Republicanism to his dying day.

John Jacob Wagenseller.

John J. Wagenseller, No. 61, page 48, was born in Selinsgrove, Snyder County, Pa., July 16, 1845. He was educated in the public schools of his native place, where he resided until the year 1862, when he moved to Bloomsburg, Columbia County, Pennsylvania. He accepted a clerkship in a general store at Bloomsburg under his brother-in-law, L. T. Sharpless. In 1865 he entered Dickinson Seminary at Williamsport where he completed his education. Returning to Bloomsburg he again entered the store as clerk and continued that occupation for two years.

Then desiring to broaden his usefulness, he accepted a position as traveling salesman throughout the central portion of Pennsylvania, for a large house in Philadelphia, at the same time making his home at No. 340 East Second Street, Bloomsburg, Columbia County, Pennsylvania.

He has continued and is yet following the same occupation. During the invasion of Pennsylvania by the confederates he was in the service of his country. In 1878 he was the senior partner in the firm of Wagenseller & Co., Jobbers in Notions, etc. He retained his connection with this business for five years. On account of too much work coupled with ill health, he sold his interest in the business and began work again on the road as a salesman. He resides at Bloomsburg, Pa. and is a member of the Methodist Episcopal Church of that place.

Dr. John Montgomery.

Dr. John Montgomery, a leading physician of Chambersburg, Franklin County, Pa., is a son of John Montgomery and Margaret Wagenseller (No. 39, page 57,) born in Brandywine Manor, Chester County, Pa., Dec. 29, 1835. He has resided in Chambersburg since 1844. After attending the common schools he was sent to the "Lititz Academy for Boys," then under the charge of John Beck, principal 1846-8. He entered the Chambersburg Academy, remained there a while, served a three years' apprenticeship in the drug business and then entered the office of Dr. John Caster Richards, a celebrated physician of Chambersburg, Pa. In October 1856 he entered Jefferson Medical College, Philadelphia and graduated March 9, 1858. He began at once to practice in Chambersburg, where he soon attained a large and lucrative practice. He was jail physician from 1860 through the war. His hospital experience was large and varied during the war, in the hospitals of his town, where large numbers of sick and wounded were cared for and the services of our home surgeons were much desired. After the burning of the town he formed a partnership with his former preceptor, Dr. J. C. Richards, Aug. 1864 which continued for more than eight years. The subject of this sketch has always pursued the practice of his profession in Chambersburg; having in 1896 associated with him his son, Dr. P. Brough Montgomery. He has been a prominent Free Mason since 1858 and is a life member of Geo. Washington Lodge, No. 143, having served as its W. Master many years. He has also been a member of Geo. Washington R. A. Chapter, No. 176, for almost forty years.

The present Medical Society of Franklin County was organized Jan. 19, 1869, the first society of 1825 having long ceased to exist. Dr. John Montgomery was one of the organizers of the present society and has been its most active worker. He has filled all the positions and is the only member who has had the honor of serving twice as president. He has been a member of Medical Society, State of Pa., since 1871, was first Vice President 1874 and 1895 and has been a Censor of his district for many years. He has also been a prominent member and frequent delegate to the American Medical Association. He was appointed by President Arthur a member of the first Board of U. S. Medical Examiners in Southern Pennsylvania, Nov. 1884 and held the position of Secretary of the Board. This he retained until March 1897, a period of 13 years, a portion of five separate National administrations. He has been for many years one of the visitors appointed by the Board of Public Charities of the State to inspect the Charitable Institutions of Franklin county.

Dr. John Montgomery married Feb. 6th, 1862, Catherine Ann, the fourth daughter of Peter Brough, who was a prominent citizen of Chambersburg. To them were born on Dec. 29, 1862 two children, Peter Brough and Margaretta and on March 23, 1875 were added to the family James H. and John Curtis. Margaretta Montgomery was born Dec. 29, 1862, died Jan. 22, 1889, aged 26 years, having passed through a beautiful life. Her unostentatious works of charity were mostly known to herself. She seemed not to live for herself alone, but always quietly hoping to help some deserving sufferer. She had never been in robust health and was the constant companion of her mother. Her death was a source of mourning and sorrow to all classes of the community, notably the afflicted and despondent class. Her remains are interred in Cedar Grove Cemetry. She made a bequest for the founding of the Teachers' Library of the Central Presbyterian

DR. JNO. MONTGOMERY,
CHAMBERSBURG, PA.   [P. 151.]

Church of which she was a member and Sunday School teacher. The growth of this Library continues by the frequent donations of books of high class, from her many loving friends. The Library was at once named *The Retta Montgomery Memorial Library.*

Peter Brough Montgomery was born at Chambersburg, Franklin County, Pa., Dec. 29, 1862 and has always resided at the place of his birth. He graduated at Public High School in 1879 and then entered the Chambersburg Academy then in charge of Prof. J. H. Shoemaker. In 1881 he took up the study of medicine in the office of his father, Dr. John Montgomery, and graduated at Bellevue Hospital Medical College of New York in 1886. He at once returned to Chambersburg, Pa. and began practice with his father, thus establishing the well-known firm of Drs. J. Montgomery & Son. In 1887 he was nominated by the Democratic party for Coroner and was elected by the largest vote ever given a Democrat in Franklin County. While Coroner he was connected with some of the most important murder trials in the history of the County. In 1892 Dr. Montgomery received the nomination at the hands of the Democratic party, for the State Legislature to represent the 33d District, composed of the counties of Franklin and Huntingdon, but was defeated in the land-slide of that year, although he ran largely ahead of his ticket. He is a member of the City Council serving a second term, having been twice elected by a handsome majority, in the Second Ward which politically is overwhelmingly against him.

Nov. 27, 1889 he married Jessie Snively, oldest daughter of E. J. Bontrake, Esq., a prominent lawyer and large real estate owner of Chambersburg, Pa. To them one son was born, William Erdman, July 12, 1892. Dr. Montgomery has been on the Staff of the Chambersburg Hospital since it was established in 1897 by the Children's Aid Society. December 1898 he entered into partnership with William G. Greenawalt, David L. Greenawalt and John C. Montgomery, forming a firm of Greenawalt &

Montgomery, wholesale and retail Drugs and Dental Supplies. This company started business by the purchase of the four largest drug stores in Chambersburg, and is to-day the largest and most substantial Drug Company in the Cumberland Valley. Although a member of this firm he continues the practice of medicine. Dr. Montgomery is prominent in Masonic circles and is a Knight Templar. In 1896 he was appointed by the State Board of Health, Medical Inspector for Franklin County. He is a member of Franklin County Medical Society, the Medical Society of State of Pennsylvania and the American Medical Association.

James Montgomery was born in Chambersburg, Pa., March 23, 1875. He was educated in the Chambersburg High School and Chambersburg Academy, studied medicine in the office of his father, attended four courses of medical lectures in Philadelphia, graduating at the Medico Chirurgical College of Philadelphia, May 31, 1898, and will in all probability locate in his native town.

John Caster Montgomery born March 23, 1875, attended the Chambersburg High School and Academy. He served apprenticeship with W. G. Greenawalt, graduated from the Philadelphia College of Pharmacy, March, 1896, passing the State Pharmacy Board and receiving the degree of Registered Pharmacist. In December, 1897, he was the promoter of the large and substantial wholesale and retail Drug Store firm of Greenawalt & Montgomery, having in possession four fine stores. They are large manufacturers and are on the jobbers' list and in consequence have advantages in large purchases and discounts. In manner affable and pleasant, possessing so many friends and the attributes of making friends, and being recognized by old business men as one of the most astute among them, his business prospects are assured. He is a Free Mason and a member of Geo. Washington Lodge, No. 143.

DR. JOHN MONTGOMERY'S ANCESTRY.

James Montgomery, our subject's grand-father, first

emigrated from the neighborhood of Ballymena County,
Antrim, Ireland in 1798. His ancestors came from Scot-
land on account of religious persecutions. They were descendants of theEglinton Branch, whose lineage is traced
to the year 900 as coming from Normandy, &c. He came
to this country a young man, locating in Chester County,
Pa., where he married Susannah Johnson Dec. 22, 1801.
He was naturalized by the Court in West Chester in 1804.
He was a successful business man having considerable estate for that day. He died in 1810, aged 50 years. Susannah, his wife, died in 1818, aged 46 years. Both are
buried at Brandywine Manor. They have two children,
James and Nancy, who married Moses Miller of Chester,
long since dead. James Montgomery was born in Chester
County, Pa. in 1808. Both parents died before he was
10 years of age and he was comparatively among strangers.
He secured a common school education, meagre of course
at that day. He was apprenticed to Alex. Marshall, a
relative, to learn the trade of harnessmaking, with whom
he served his time. He married Margaretta, daughter of
Jacob Wagenseller. (Record lost in the burning of Chambersburg.) They lived for a short time at Rising Sun,
Lancaster County and at Brandywine Manor, Chester
County. They had two children, Hannah Ann, who died
in infancy and our subject. James Montgomery left Chester County in the Spring of 1837, having purchased a
small farm in Letterkenny township, Franklin County,
Pa. Soon after he exchanged this property to Christian
Bilger for a Wayside Iron in Upper Strasburg, Franklin
County, which was at that time on one of the great thor-
oughfares of travel for the large droves of stock of all kinds
going east. In 1844 he disposed of this property, sojourn-
ing for six months at Shippensburg and in Sept. 1844
purchased and occupied the large hotel property in Chambersburg north of the Center Square on the main street of
the town which was enlarged and improved. This property, known as the Montgomery House, remained in the
family for 50 years. It was recently disposed of by the

estate for a large price, being one of the most valuable properties in the town. This was the second change in owners in over 100 years. This property was all destroyed in the burning of Chambersburg, July 30th, 1864, by the Rebel Cavalry under Gen. McCausland, the loss to this estate approximating $20,000. A large four-story building was quickly reared and leased as hotel and stores. James Montgomery, who was always held as a man of sterling qualities, died March 17, 1858. Margaretta Montgomery, one of the best known and universally beloved women in the country, died June 1st, 1876 and with her husband is interred in Cedar Grove Cemetery.

The ancestry of Dr. Montgomery can be traced back to Roger de Montgomery of Normandy who lived about 900. Unfortunately, the name of his great-grand-father is missing, which must form the connecting link. This family were Presbyterians and this is the reason, the ancestors left their native heath on the land of the Scots. The ancestry includes: HUGH d. 1545, the first Earl of Eglinton titled by King James IV, 1507-8; son of ALEXANDER, d. prior to 1484, second Lord of Montgomery; son of ALEXANDER, d. 1452, Master of Montgomery; son of ALEXANDER, d. 1461 first Lord of Montgomery, titled by James II, 1448-9; son of Sir JOHN of Androssan d. prior to 1429; son of Sir JOHN of Eaglesham; son of Sir ALEXANDER of Eaglesham, knighted by Robert Bruce; son of Sir JOHN of Eaglesham; son of Sir JOHN of Eaglesham; son of ALAN of Eaglesham; son of Sir JOHN of Eaglesham; son of ROBERT of Eaglesham; son of PHILIP; son of ARNULPH, d. 1119, Earl of Pembroke; son of ROGER, Count of Montgomery, commanded the vanguard of William the Conqueror's army in the battle of Hastings 1066; son of HUGH D. de M.; son of WILLIAM de M.; son of ROGER de M.; son of ROGER de Montgomery of Normandy.

J. B. EVANS,
UWCHLAN, PA.   [P. 159.]

Jesse Benner Evans.

The subject here named represents a character doubly related to the Wagenseller family. He is the husband of Sarah Susannah Wagenseller (see No. 55, page 71) and a descendant of Catherine Wagenseil and Conrad King. He is a native of Uwchlan township, Chester County, Pennsylvania and spent his early years on a farm, having been educated in the public schools. He taught school a while but being not congenial to his taste, he abandoned the calling. He studied dentistry with W. P. Lambert of Philadelphia and for three years practiced at Phoenixville, then returned to farming in Upper Uwchlan township, where he has resided ever since. He was married in 1850, not 1851, as stated on page 71, where a full list of his childred and grand-children will be found. Being reared in the Democratic faith, he voted that ticket until the trouble created by a stubborn desire to force slavery on the people of Kansas. He, being naturally opposed to slavery, left the democratic party and has since been acting in harmony with the principles of the Republican party. January 22, 1853 he received the degree of an Entered Apprenticed Mason in Phoenixville Lodge, No. 75 and on February 19, was passed to the degree of a Fellow Craft Mason and March 19, was raised to the degree of Master Mason. He subsequently resigned his membership and assisted in the organization of Lodge, No. 446, of which he is still a member. In November 1859, he was baptized into the Fellowship of Windsor Baptist Chnrch. Frequently he has been treasurer, deacon and trustee of the congregation.

He has been a school director for ten years and a justice-of-
the-peace for two terms in a township where his political
party is in a hopeless minority.   Feeling the weight of
more than three score years and ten, he has been compelled
to cease the active labors of life, resigning them to younger
men.   His postoffice address is Uwchlan, Chester County,
Pa.

Benjamin Franklin Evans,

Is a native of Phoenixville, Pa.. the son of J. B. and Sarah S. [Wagenseller] Evans. He was educated in the public schools of Upper Uwchlan township and at Millersville State Normal School. At the age of 19 he went to Philadelphia where he remained until January 1, 1876. The year following he spent as traveling salesman for a Notion Firm in Bloomsburg, Pa. April 1, 1877 he began farming. In March 1877, he moved to Downingtown and was employed in a planing mill until Jan. 5, 1895 when he bought the Coal, Wood and Lumber Business, he now controls. In February 1898 he formed a partnership with C. E. Walker for the manufacture of Ladies' hosiery. In February 1891, he was elected Tax Collector of the Borough of Downingtown and has been re-elected ever since, consequently at present holding the office. Post Office, East Downingtown, Chester County, Pennsylvania.

Prof. Wilbur F. Gearhart.

Wilbur Fisk Gearhart, a son of the late Rev. Franklin Gearhart and Mary Elizabeth Wagenseller Gearhart, was born in Hanover, Pa., June 18, 1868. As a baby he was very delicate and suffered severely from pneumonia during the first year of his existence, but by careful nursing and hygienic training he developed into a strong and robust boy, and at the present writing he is an all-round athletic and physical instructor of considerable ability.

As a child he attended the public schools in various Pennsylvania towns, and afterwards took a special scientific course at the Dickinson Seminary of Williamsport, Pa. He graduated at the Brooklyn Normal School of Physical Education in the spring of 1890 and has since that time taken a Special Anatomical Course at the Louisville, Ky. Medical College. After finishing his course at Brooklyn he accepted a flattering offer from the Louisville Athletic Club, the membership of which was composed of the cream of Louisville's society people. He remained in charge of the above club three years and four months, establishing an excellent reputation as a gentleman, an athlete and instructor. After leaving the Louisville Athletic Club he opened a private Academy of Physical Culture of his own and in addition accepted the instructorship of the Y. M. H. A. of Louisville, and that institution has flourished greatly under his instructions. On his 24th birthday, June 18, 1892, he wedded Miss Anna Middendorf, a tall, handsome and popular Louisville belle who has made an excellent wife. His abilities as an athlete and physical

instructor, as well as his moral and mental attainments, have been recognized not only by his immediate associates, but also by the public press throughout the country.

As an athlete he has a record of which our family can be proud. He has achieved a record for a double foot high kick of 7 feet, 6 inches. In making this sort of a jump, the athlete must keep his feet side by side without any turn over, kicking the object with both feet at the same time and alighting on the floor on both feet at once, no other part of the person touching the floor. It is a most difficult feat and one that few athletes can accomplish without a great deal of practice. He has been mainly instrumental in bringing into prominence several amateur athletes whose names are now known throughout the East and the South, and as he is not yet in his prime, and is completely wrapped up in his profession, he will doubtless long continue to perform yeoman's service in the field of physical culture to which he is by nature and inclination so well adapted.

Joseph Marshall.

Joseph Mashall, son of John Marshall and Thamzen Wagenseller, (No. 18, page 45) was born August 17, 1821, in Wilmington, Delaware. Among Joseph's early recollections is his father's hurrahing for General Jackson. His first schooling was obtained in his native place. When he was nine years of age, he went to live with Benjamin Chandler in the state of Delaware where he remained until he was sixteen years of age. He was to have three months' schooling each year, but he seldom received one. He went to the state of Ohio in 1837 to learn the molding trade with his uncle, George Marshall, of Madisonville. His uncle failed and then brought young Joseph to Cincinnati, Ohio, and from there he moved to Batavia, Clearmount County, Ohio, where he now resides. There he lived with his uncle, Edward Marshall, for a short time. He went to learn the carpenter trade with William Lytle and worked for him about six years, then entered a partnership and has since followed his trade up to within the last few years. He was married first in 1845 to Rebecca Leads, who died in 1856 and second in 1857 he married Rebecca Ann Ross who died in 1880 and third on Dec. 29, 1884 to Frances Butler. With his first wife he had seven children, Ruth Elizabeth, born 1845, now the wife of Rev. G. D. Gross of Colburn, Ind.; Susan Agnes, widow of William S. Moore of Baltimore, Md.; George M. and John M. died in manhood; Thamzen, Iona, Thressa and Viola died in infancy and Alfred A., who now resides in DeLamar, Nevada. With his second wife he had three children, Oliver Freeman, born Sept. 17, 1859 and died Feb. 8, 1891 ; Thallie Victor, born October 26, 1861 ; Daniel Lyman, born 1863 and died in 1864 when about 16 months old. There has been no issue with his third wife. Joseph Marshall has eight grand-children living and one great-grand-child. None of his children are now living in Ohio and none of his grand-children live there except a little daughter of Oliver Freeman Marshall, who was named Olive after her father.

Our subject has played a prominent part in the community in which he resides. He was township trustee from 1862 to 1864, has been a member of the Board of Education for the last twenty years and still holds the position. For forty-eight years he has been a member of the Masonic Fraternity and he is now the past-master of Batavia Lodge No. 104. He never voted for a democrat except William J. Bryan. He belonged to the Militia, went to Camp Denilson, slept on a board for two nights and was then discharged for disability. Joseph Marshall or "Uncle Joe" as he is familiarly called, is in his 77th year, is tall, straight as a boy and will always be like a boy as long as he lives. The boys and girls love this old man and say there is more fun in him than in those of younger years.

P. S. His father died in Williamsport, Indiana. Joseph's house was destroyed by fire April 19, 1898.

William H. Young.

William H. Young, first son of John and Margaret Hohrnetter [Wagenseller] Young, see No. 34, page 38, was born in Philadelphia and when quite young removed to Charlestown township, Chester County, Penna. A few years later, 1851, the family moved to West Pikeland. When William grew into youth and manhood he attended the Freeland Seminary in Montgomery County for two years, then spent several years teaching school and traveling. His wife died at Lionville in 1895 at the age of 47 years. He lived at Lionville from 1893 to 1896, then removed to his present residence, the old Rising Sun farm and tavern, the family homestead along the old Conestoga Road. At this place his grand-father, William Wagenseller, spent so many years of his life keeping tavern and farming.

In politics he has adhered to the principles of the democratic party. He was twice elected justice-of-the-peace, and several times school director of his district and has held minor offices in his township. He is not wealthy, but is one of the active and progressive men in the community. He is ever ready to lend a helping hand to enhance the interests of the community which was so highly honored by his much esteemed ancestors.

The Royer Connection.

In describing character No. 8 on page 28, we were totally ignorant of Benjamin Royer, the husband of Anna Maria Wagenseller, or Mary Wagenseller as she was called in the home, and even now we are not over-burdened with information concerning him. We are told without proof that the father of Benjamin Royer, is Michael Royer (Reyer.) Michael Royer was born about 1844. married April 24, 1864 to Rosina Seybert. They were the parents of at least five children: (1) Michael Royer, who was married Dec. 11, 1796 to Eva Schweinhard; (2) Rebecca Royer, who was married Nov. 25, 1804 to George Spatz ; (3) Catherine Royer married about 1800 to David Roth ; (4) Benjamin Royer, our central subject, born 1769, married about 1792 to Mary Wagenseller and died in 1823. His widow died in 1845 at the age of 75 years ; (5) David.

It seems that Benjamin Royer and his wife, Mary Wagenseller, left a family of eight children : (1) Their oldest son, John H. Royer, was born in Limerick township, Montgomery County, Pa., Feb. 22, 1792 and died very suddenly, March 17, 1875 in Phoenixville, Pa. He was married in 1821 to Rachael Lesher of Pottstown. Having been quite prominent in his day, he was editor of several different newspapers at various times and places. Mrs. A. F. Borden of Philadelphia is a daughter of John and Rachael. Benjamin and Mary's other children were (2) George, (3) Rosanna, (4) Margaret, (5) Sarah, (6) Samuel, (7) Maria and (8) Benjamin, Jr.

When Benjamin Royer died in 1823 the widow,

Mary Wagenseller, and her eldest son, John H. Royer, were the administrators of Benjamin Royer's Estate. June 5, 1801, Benjamin Royer of Chester County purchased land adjoining David Royer.

Having disposed of the meager information concerning the descendants of Benjamin Royer, we must look after his ancestry. If Michael Royer is the father of Benjamin, as stated, Michael must be the eldest son of Johann Carl, who is the son of John Michael Reyer, described on pages 28-9. Johann Carl Reyer is a son of the first marriage, born Dec. 15, 1711, married Elizabeth ———. He lived in Providence Twp., Montgomery, Co., Pa., where he owned at his death a plantation of 150 acres of land. He was known as Colder Royer and Charles Royer. He died Oct. 29, 1780 and is buried in the Trappe Lutheran burying ground. The plantation was valued at £785, gold and silver, lawful money of Pennsylvania and the widow's dower was £15 13 4 yearly. Michael Reyer, the oldest son, the father of Benjamin, took the plantation. We should say here that we have no proof for saying that Michael the son of Carl is the same Michael that is the father of Benjamin, but circumstantial evidence points that way. We feel positive that this is the true condition. The following extracts from the records of Philadelphia give particulars as to the land owned by Carl Royer and afterward by Michael Royer.

September 6, 1735, John Penn, Thomas Penn and Richard Penn, the proprietaries granted to James Steel two thousand acres of land situate on the northeast side of the River Schuylkill, adjoining the Manor Gilberts, under a yearly quit rent of one shilling sterling for every hundred acres.

James Steel in his lifetime sold, but did not actually convey, to Colder Royer a part of the foregoing tract for £150, of which £24 was paid. On the 9th of January, 1745, the heirs and legatees of James steel (he having died) conveyed to Colder Royer, of Providence township, in fulfillment of the foregoing bargain, one hundred and fifty acres and forty-seven perches, situate in Providence township, and bounded as follows : Beginning at a post in a line of land lately granted to George Moyer, thence by Philip Sitsler's and David Phillip's lands southeast 139 perches to a post, thence by Jacob Nutt's land southwest 173 perches to a post, thence by lands of Jacob Cough and George Burson northwest 139 perches to a post, thence the lands of Conrad Rabell and George Moyer northeast 173 perches to the place of beginning.

Descendants of John and Esther [Zerbe] Forry.

Mrs. Rebecca Wagenseller, widow of William Jeremiah Wagenseller (No. 77) is the daughter of John Forry (Forrer) and Esther Zerbe, who were married in Berks County, Pennsylvania, by Rev. Thomas Leinbach, October 28, 1832. John Forrer (it is so spelled in his German Bible dated 1833) was born March 25, 1805 in Berks County, Penna., probably in Heidleburg township. Esther Zerbe, his wife, was born Nov. 20, 1814 in Berks County, Pa., and died in Penn township, Snyder County, Pa., August 27, 1874, aged 59 years, 9 months and 7 days. John Forry died in Penn township, January 2, 1865 aged 58 years, 8 months and 24 days. John Forrer moved from Berks County, Pa., to Perry township, Union County, about 1840. The district is now West Perry township, Snyder County, near Richfield, Juniata County. He was a fuller and conducted a woolen mill there for several years. He then moved to the Island near Kantz, in Penn township, Snyder County and continued in the same business for several years. The march of progress brought later devices for the manufacture of woolen goods and consequently he abandoned the business and went to farming. The mill he then occupied, was destroyed by fire about 1874-5. Leaving here, he moved to a farm near Duck's mill, halfway between Freeburg and Kantz, then to Boyer's farm along Middlecreek and finally to Col. Henry C. Eyer's farm in Penn township, ½ mile below Selinsgrove, where he remained until he died in 1865. His last will and testament dated September 9, 1864, probated February 20, 1865 is on file in the Middleburg Court House. John and Esther Forry were the parents of sixteen children, most of whom have grown into manhood and womanhood, are all living, are all married but one and nearly all have grand-children. Their list of children are as follows:

1. Edward Forry, born in Berks County, Pa., August 23, 1833, baptized by Rev. Fred Herman. Sponsors, George and Magdalena Forrer. George, the sponsor, was an uncle of Edward's father, who possessed a large estate and died without immediate heirs and the distribution of his estate became the bone of contention in the courts until the estate was very nearly parcelled out in attorney fees and costs. Edward now resides at Freeburg, Snyder Co., Pa. He was married December 18, 1859 by by Rev. A. B. Casper to Sarah Ann Jodon, who was born May 10, 1836. He is a carpet weaver of ability. They are the parents of four children:

      i. B. Franklin, born April 14, 1860, married Sept. 5, 1880 to Amanda Elizabeth Moyer. They reside in Selinsgrove and have five children, Edward Nathaniel, born June 20, 1881; Mabel May, born Jan. 28, 1885 and died Sept. 2. 1891; Chas. Arthur, born Feb. 11, 1891; Howard, born March 13, 1893, and Roy born Nov. 26, 1894.

     ii. Simon Peter, born Aug. 2, 1862.

    iii. John Thomas, born June 2, 1866.

    iv. Mary Effie, born Oct. 13, 1871, married to Joseph Roush.

2. John Forry, born in Berks County, Penna., Sept. 28, 1834, baptized by Rev. William Hendel. Sponsors, John and Maria Stub. The latter is a sister of John Forry's father. John resides at Elkhart, Ind., has a large

family and quite a list of grand-children.   Quite a number of unsuccessful requests were made for data cencerning them.

3. Levi Forry, born May 29, 1836, baptized by Rev. William Hendel. Sponsors, Isaac and Rebecca Noll. Died young.

4. Amanda Forry, born in Berks County, September 29, 1837, baptized by Rev. William Hendel. Sponsors, Daniel and Harriet Fisher.   Married Lt. William H. Gemberling, born Sept. 22, 1837, and they live at Selinsgrove, Pa. They have had eight children. Two of them Anna and Charles are dead. The living are:

    i. Esther, born April 20, 1856, married Feb. 15, 1873 to Harry L. Noll, who was born Aug. 7, 1850. They reside at Myerstown, Lebanon County, Pa. and have two children, E. Bertha, born Sept. 23, 1873 and William H., born Nov. 20, 1875, is married and has one child dead.

    ii. Calvin Augustus, born August 3, 1858, married June 5, 1879 to Mary C. Miller, daughter of John J. Miller of Selinsgrove. They reside at Mifflinburg and have ten children, Blanche, Harry, Maude, Edwin, Paul, Susie and an infant son, who are living. Irwin, a twin to Edwin and a pair of twins are dead.

    iii. Lydia Amelia, born June 11, 1863 married Sept. 1, 1885, to Perry L. Romig. He is a bridge builder of great skill. His permanent address is Selinsgrove, Pa. They have one son, William Isaac, born May 27.

iv. Martha Jane, born Nov. 27, 1870, married Flem. Seesholtz of Sunbury. Their first child, a daughter, is dead, the second a son, Eugene Schroyer, is living. They reside at Sunbury.

v. Jeneatte Bell, born Jan. 10, 1872, married July 17, 1890 to Newton Absalom Bowes, born Aug. 8, 1868. They reside at Middleburgh, Pa. and have had six children, Amanda, born Sept. 4, 1891; Twins, Minerva Mary and Esther Lagotta, born Nov. 26, 1893, died the same day; Joseph Robert, born July 9. 1895; Paul Snyder, born Jan. 8, 1897 and an infant son born June 6, 1898.

vi. Agnes May, born Oct. 2, 1877, married Nov. 12, 1896 to James F. Moyer. They reside at Selinsgrove and have one son, Perry Fisher, born June, 1897.

5. Jonathan Forry born in Berks County, Penna., Nov. 22, 1838, baptized by Rev. Hendel. Sponsors, Jonathan and Maria Klopp. Mrs. Klopp is a cousin of Jonathan Forry's father and Mr. Klopp at one time owned the large grist mill in Selinsgrove, now in the possession of Howard Davis Schnure. Jonathan Forry formerly resided in Penn township, Snyder County, but for the last 15 years he has resided at Milton, Pa. He married, 1861, Deborah Grissinger, who was born in Northumberland County, May 1, 1841 and was baptized by Rev. Shindel. They have had born to them a family of ten children:

i. Charles Albert, born in Snyder County, was twice married, his first wife having died. He has several children, resides at McKees Half

Falls, Snyder County and is proprietor of the hotel at that place.

ii. Clara Elizabeth, born Jan. 3, 1864, baptized by Rev. Hottenstein in Snyder County, married Feb. 29, 1884 to George B. Shoemaker. They reside at Milton, Pa., and have two children, Jennie Bartley, born Jan. 8, 1885 and Frank, born April 3, 1891.

iii. Anna, born Aug. 2, 1865 in Snyder County, baptized by Rev. Hottenstein, married Oct. 11, 1888 to James D. Mumma of Milton, Pa. They are the parents of three children, Harriet Deborah, born May 3, 1889; Sarah, born Aug. 10, 1890 and Joel Benton born Sept. 8, 1892 and died Dec. 8, 1895.

iv. John Harvey, born May 9, 1867, baptized in Snyder County by Rev. Hottenstein.

v. William Oliver, born November 15, 1868 in Snyder County, baptized by Rev. Hottenstein, married Feb. 10, 1895 to Amanda Felmy to whom was born Oct. 3, 1895, a daughter named Ruth.

vi. Sarah Albertha, born in Snyder County, Aug. 31, 1870, married Jan. 3, 1890 to Frank Munson. They have 5 children, George Lee, born Aug. 1, 1891; Wm. Ray, born Oct. 24, 1892; Ella Jeneatta, born April 10, 1894; Charles, born July 12, 1895 and Jennie May born Jan. 8, 1877.

vii. Martha Jeneatte, born in Snyder

County April 30, 1872 and was baptized by Rev. Hause.

viii. Forest Meaker, born in Snyder County, April 10, 1874 and was baptized by Rev. Hause.

ix. Jeremiah Foster, born in Snyder County, Jan. 28, 1876.

x. Lillian May, born in Snyder County, Oct. 5, 1879, was baptized by Rev. J. M. Reimensnyder and died Nov. 10, 1889.

6. Rebecca Forry, born near Richfield, within the limits of Snyder (then Union) County, Pa., Nov. 20, 1840, baptized by Rev. Seibert. Sponsors, the parents. Married Nov. 5, 1861 to William Jeremiah Wagenseller, with whom she had ten children, as follows:

i. Kate Alice, born Feb. 22, 1862, is unmarried and a milliner at Selinsgrove.

ii. Mary Louisa, born May 17, 1864 and died Aug. 25, 1865.

iii. John Franklin, born Aug. 1, 1866.

iv. George Washington, born April 27, 1868. Married Oct. 22, 1896 to Miriam Orwig, daughter of Dr. John W. and Margaret [Zellers] Orwig. Residence, Middleburg, Pa.

v. Infant son, born April 28, 1870 and died May 6, 1870.

vi. Ida May, born May 15, 1870.

vii. Amon Sylvester, born Nov. 11, 1873. Married August 8, 1897 to Jeneatte Smith. They have a son, Bruce Sylvester, born February 23, 1898. Residence, Selinsgrove, Pa.

viii. Anna Celesta, born June 10, 1876 and died Feb. 17, 1882.

ix.   Charles Henry, born Dec. 9, 1877
      and died July 24, 1878.
x.   Infant son, born Sept 30, 1881 and
      died same day.

7.   William Forry, born March 11, 1842, baptized
by Rev. Seibert, now deceased.

8.   Alfred Forry, born July 20, 1843, a cripple,
baptized by Rev. Seibert, a Reformed minister, and died
August 19, 1879, aged 36 years and 29 days.

9.   Elmira Forry, born Oct. 29, 1844, in Union
(now Snyder) County, was married first to Mathias U.
App, July 6, 1873, now deceased, and second, Feb. 25,
1896, to David Reed, born June 10, 1839, now reside at
Adamsville, Cass County, Michigan.   M. U. App was
first married to Matilda Bealer. Gertrude Irene, a daughter of Elmira, born May 9, 1862, was married by Rev. H.
B. Belmer, Jan, 1, 1878 to Samuel L. App, a son of M.
U. and Matilda App, born Oct. 31, 1850.   To Samuel
and Gertrude App are born three children, Anna Merinda,
born Nov. 3, 1879, died Sept 18, 1880; Harry, born Jan.
15, 1881 and Susan Elmira born Oct. 2, 1883.

10.   Lydia Forry, born in Washington township,
Sept. 19, 1846, baptized by Rev. Leise, married Norman
Fisher.   She has a daughter, Minnie, married to William
Hughes, a prominent attorney at Missoula, Montana. They
have a son, Arthur, now resides at Alvira, Union County,
Pa.   A daughter Hattie and other children reside at home
on the old Fisher homestead on the Isle of Que, two miles
south of Selinsgrove, Pa.

11.   Mary Ann Forry, born in Washington township, Oct. 21, 1848, baptized by Rev. Leise. Sponsors,
parents.   Married by Rev. C. G. Erlenmeyer, March 9,
1875 to Jocob Martin, who was born January 12, 1852
and now resides at Goshen, Indiana.   They have five children :

i.   Hattie Jane, born Sept. 25, 1875.
ii.   Barbara Ellen, born Dec. 8, 1876,
      now deceased.

 iii. William Newton, born May 17, 1878, now dead.

 iv. Nettie Dora, born Nov. 18, 1879.

 v. Anna Mabel, born Sept. 8, 1886.

 12. Elizabeth Forry, born in Washington township, Sept. 9, 1850, baptized by Rev. Leise, married Nov. 3, 1867 to W. N. Fisher, who was born Oct. 10, 1846, and now resides on the Isle of Que, about 2½ miles south of Selinsgrove. To them have been born six children :

 i. Lydia Dora, born Jan. 23, 1869.

 ii. John Christian, born Sept. 9, 1870, and died Jan. 23, 1871.

 iii. Franklin Foster, born Jan. 18, 1872.

 iv. Carrie Olevia, born Aug. 12, 1873.

 v. Dennis Roscoe, born Aug. 17, 1875.

 vi. Edna May, born May 14, 1878.

 13. Samuel Boyer Forry, born in Snyder (then Union) County, Pa., Aug. 25, 1852, unmarried. Resides with Mrs. Sarah Fisher, on Isle of Que, near Selinsgrove.

 14. A son, born Jan. 12, 1854, died in infancy.

 15. Calvin Forry, born Feb. 28, 1855, baptized by Rev. Leise, married Oct. 29, 1874 by Rev. C. G. Erlenmeyer to Alice Daubert of Port Treverton, Pa., who was born July 18, 1857. They now reside near Kantz, Snyder County. They have two children :

 i. Sarah S., born July 10, 1875, married July 22, 1894 to Forest E. Holtzapple.

 ii. George Robert, born Aug. 24, 1878.

 16. Catherine Forry, born Nov. 25, 1857, baptized by Rev. Erlenmeyer. Sponsors, Conrad and Catherine Fetter. She married Frank Duck. They have a son, Foster, and reside near Kantz, Snyder County, Pa.

 We stated that John Forrer and his wife Esther Zerbe came from Berks County to Snyder (then Union) County, Pa., 1839-40. As their children were baptized by Revs.

Herman and Hendel, pastor of St. John's Reformed church in Heidleburg township, Berks County, we infer they resided near there. The church is known as Hain's church and is located one mile north of Wernersville. This congregation was organized about 1732 and hence it is one of the oldest in Berks County. The present pastor of the church is Rev. W. J. Kerchner, No. 115 South Third St., Reading, Pa.

The ancestry of John Forrer and Esther Zerbe has not been traced. There were two immigrants to Pennsylvania. Johannes Forrer, (Page 11, Pennsylvania Archives, Vol. XVII) arrived in the Ship Friendship of Bristol, John Davies, Master from Rotterdam, qualified at Philadelphia Oct. 16, 1727. On page 432, the same volume, we learn that Johannes Forrer arrived in the Ship Brothers, Capt. William Muir from Rotterdam, qualified Sept. 30, 1754. This is probably the grand-father of John Forry for we learn (page 335, Vol. II, Pa. Archives) that Johannes Forrer of Berks County took the oath of allegiance, March 30, 1755.

NOTES.

Zerbe.—They came over land from Schoharie, N. Y. to Tulpekocken, Berks County, Pa., and settled in the Weiser colony 1723-7. They were a prominent family.

Peter Sarvey, probably Zerbe came from Albany, N. Y. to Tulpehocken, Berks County, Pa. in 1723.

1756.—Jacob Zerbe is named a referee in the docket of Peter Spyker, Esq., at Tulpehocken.

1779.—John Zerbe, Michael Furer (Forrer), Christian Zerbe, Benjamin Zerbe and Daniel Zerbe of Berks County, Pa., signed a petition against calling a convention to amend the constitution of the state.

March 24, 1782.—Jacob Zerbe married Maria Kline. *Historical Register.*

These notes are given for the benefit of those who may wish to continue the search.

The Orwig Genealogy.

This chapter on the Orwig genealogy is an after consideration and was not originally intended for this history and hence at this late period it is impossible to make it complete. We will give it as complete as possible in accordance with our statement on page 111.

1. GOTTFRIED[1] ORWIG.—The founder of the name in America was Gottfried Orwig, born, it is supposed, in Brunswick, Germany, August 24th, 1719, and was among those whose names are given as qualifying October 2nd, 1741, arriving at the port of Philadelphia from Rotterdam in the ship St. Andrew, Charles Stedman, Master. His age is given in the list as 22, which agrees with the tombstone record at Orwigsburg. Owing to the large influx or foreigners, it was deemed advisable to compell all to take oath of allegiance to King George II. Accordingly, all males over sixteen years of age were compelled to take the oath, and as soon as they were landed were marched to the Court House for that purpose. (See copy of oath in preface to Pennsylvania Archives compiled by W. H. Egle, State Librarian; also see Rupp's 30,000 emigrants into Pennsylvania, page 148. Also, see page 213 Pennsylvania Archives Second Series, Vol. 17.)

Rev. J. B. Orwig of Ellsworth, Kansas, in a letter dated March 19th, 1896, says : "Great-grand-father, Gottfried, stayed in America a few years and then went back to Germany when, after a few years' visit returned to America, bringing with him his wife, Clara, maiden name unknown. During the Revolutionary War a company of old

men was organized, Germans, eighty in all. (See cottage
Cyclopedia, page 695.) It was called the Old Men's Company. Their captain was nearly one hundred years old,
drummer ninety-four, the youngest nearly seventy. In a
history of Pennsylvania the names of this company are giv-
en and Gottfried is among them. This surely is my great-
grand-father."

Gottfried Orwig and wife settled at a place called
Maiden Creek, near Reading, Penna. in 1743, on lands
purchased from the Iroquois Indians but afterwards removed to Sculp Hill, one mile south of the present town
of Orwigsburg in Schuylkill County. He and his wife
were buried in the old Lutheran Church Yard at the foot
of Sculp Hill, opposite the old red church. Their tombstones have the following inscriptions :

Hier ruhet	Translation.
GOTTFRIED ORWIG,	Here rests
Geboren den 24 August	GOTTFRIED ORWIG,
1719,	born August 24th, 1719,
Starb den 26 May	died May 26th, 1804,
1804.	age 85 years,
Alt 85 jahr, weniger 2 monat.	less 2 months.

Hier ruhet	Translation.
CLARA ORWIG,	Here rests
Ehefrau des	CLARA ORWIG,
GOTTFRIED ORWIG,	wife of
Geboren	GOTTFRIED ORWIG,
den 26 January, 1716,	born
Starb	January 26th, 1716,
den 5 January, 1788.	died January 5th, 1788,
Alt 72 jahr,	age 72 years,
weniger 3 woche.	less three weeks.

The children of Gottfried and Clara Orwig are as
follows :

2.   i.   Catharine, born Dec. 4, 1748.
+3.   ii. Peter, born at Maiden Creek, Berks
                     County, Penna., July 8th, 1750,

died at Orwigsburg about 1807, married to Hannah Webb. Dates of her birth and their marriage unknown. She died about 1831 at the home of her daughter, Sarah Hoover, in Milesburg, Penna. and was buried in Milesburg.

4.   iii.   Maria, born December 19th, 1751.

5.   iv.   Henry, born at Maiden Creek, December 6th, 1753 ; married Elizabeth Haring (No children.) Was private soldier in the Revolutionary War, in Col. William Thompson's Riflemen, Capt. Geo. Nagle's Company, one year from June 1775; afterwards he was an Ensign of the Second Company, 4th Battalion Berks County Militia, commissioned May 10th, 1780. Was in the skirmishes about Boston, and later in the battle of Brandywine ; died December 18th, 1836, and was buried at Orwigsburg.

6.   v.   Elizabeth, born October 8th, 1756.

+7.   vi.   George, born March 11, 1758. Of Catherine, Maria and Elizabeth, daughters of Gottfried, nothing is known but their names and dates of birth.

3.   PETER², (*Gottfried¹*), born July 8, 1750, married Hannah Webb. He assisted his father to found the town of Orwigsburg in 1796 as did the other sons, Henry and George. The children of Peter and Hannah Orwig are :

8.   i.   Maria Rebecca, born April 17, 1774, married ———— Miller.

9.   ii.   John Henry, born Dec. 27, 1775.

+10.   iii.   Samuel, born Oct. 3, 1779.

11.	iv.	Esther, born Oct. 14, 1788, married Wm. Boggs of Milesburg, Pa.
12.	v.	Sarah, married Jacob Hoover of Brush Valley, Pa.
13.	vi.	Henry, lived in Schuylkill County.
14.	vii.	Elizabeth, born Aug. 25, 1790.
+15.	viii.	Jacob, born May 25, 1792.
16.	ix.	John, lived in Wheeling.
17.	x.	Joseph (youngest) died at Akron, O. Left two sons and two daughters.
18.	xi.	Mary, married ——— Silar.

7. GEORGE², (*Gottfried¹*), born March 11, 1758. He is the youngest child and was born at Maiden Creek, near Reading, Pa.

In July, 1776 enlisted and served five months in the Rifle Company, commanded by Capt. James Olds, and during this service was engaged in the battle of Long Island, and in the battle at White Plains; In August, 1777, he enlisted as a substitute for Philip Shots, and served two months as a private in the company commanded by Capt. Jacob Whetstone, and was engaged in the battle of Brandywine; In the winter of 1778 enlisted as a substitute for his brother, Henry Orwig, and served one month as a private at Plymouth Meeting, about twelve miles from Philadelphia; In March and April of the same year served two months as a private at White Marsh about ten miles from Philadelphia, under the command of Col. Lindamute and Lt. Col. George May; In Sept. 1778, served about two months at Ft. Jenkins, as a private under the officers last named. He married Maria Magdalen Gilbert,(daughter of Conrad Gilbert) born Aug. 10, 1758; died Jan. 30, 1841. George Orwig died March 2, 1841, at Mifflinburg, Pa.

George Orwig was appointed Ensign in the 6th Company, second Battalion, Berks County Militia, April 21, 1783. (See Penna. Archives Vol. 10, page 191).

SOME GILBERT DATA.

Conrad Gilbert, the father of Mrs. George Orwig, is represented as a "taylor" who bought, January 27, 1761, from Ludwig Hering of Douglass township, Montgomery County, Pa., 23 acres and 32 perches of land partly in McCall's Manor. Conrad Gilbert and his wife Anna Elizabeth ———— had children as follows:

1. Mary Magdalena, born Aug. 10, 1758, baptized by the pastor of the New Hanover Lutheran Church, Sept. 3, 1758. Sponsors, Adam Brobst and wife.

2. Catherine, born Sept. 2, 1760, baptized Sept. 28, 1760. Sponsors, Andrew Yoerger and wife.

3. Anna Elizabeth, born Aug. 25, 1762, baptized Sept. 12, 1762. Sponsors, Andrew Yerger and wife.

4. Andrew, born Sept. 26, 1764, baptized Oct. 21, 1764. Sponsors, Andrew Yerger and wife, Catherine.

5. John Peter, born July 25, 1766, baptized Aug. 17, 1766. Sponsors, John P. Steltz and Susanna Kuhle (Keely.)

6. Anna Maria, (?) born Dec. 23, 1770, baptized Jan. 13, 1771. Sponsors, John George Schweinhard and wife Anna Maria.

7. Salome Gilbert born Dec. 9, 1772, baptized Dec. 25, 1772. Sponsors, George Gilbert and wife Maria Salome.

8. Christina Gilbert, born Sept. 29, 1775, baptized Oct. 15, 1775. Sponsors, Henry Gilbert and wife, Christina.

———

The Gilbert family in Falkner Swamp was a numerous one and is hard to trace and if my readers will pardon the allusion in this connection to Barnerd Gilbert mentioned on page 17, time may perhaps evolve the discovery of the relationship between Conrad and Bernard Gilbert, both of whom took the oath of allegience on the same day,— Sept. 23, 1760. There were two persons by the name of Barned Gilbert, which does not lessen the confusion of the

Gilbert aggregation, but the Bernard who took the oath of allegiance the same day with Conrad must have been Bernard Gilbert, Sr., married to Mary Elizabeth Meyer. This couple is the father of Bernard Gilbert, born March 9, 1766, baptized by the pastor of the New Hanover Lutheran Church, March 30, 1766. Sponsors, Henry Schirm and wife, Magdalena; married Susanna ———, perhaps Hornetter, as Andrew Hornetter had a daughter Susanna and Bernard Gilbert was one of the executors of the will of Andrew Hornetter as was also John Wagenseller, a son-in-law. When the exact relationship is proven, as it doubtless can, it will show a relationship between the Orwig's and the Wagensellers of the Revolutionary period through the Gilberts. Bernard and Susanna Gilbert had children :

1. Henry, born Sept. 24, 1791, baptized by the pastor of the New Hanover Lutheran Church Oct. 9, 1791. Sponsors, Bernard and wife, Mary Elizabeth.

2. Magdalena, born Feb. 7, 1797, baptized Feb. 11, 1797. Sponsors, Bernard Gilbert, Sr. and wife.

3. John, born Nov. 7, 1801, baptized Jan. 3, 1802. Sponsors, John Adam Gilbert and wife Magdaleda.

4. George, born Nov. 8, 1803, baptized January 29, 1804. Sponsors, John Gilbert and wife, Elizabeth.

The author believes that the relationship here suggested between the Gilberts, Wagensellers and Orwigs, can, and will some day be solved.

George Orwig, about the year 1812 moved from Berks County, to Union County, Pennsylvania and settled near Mifflinburg. Both he and his wife are lying in the old burying-ground at Mifflinburg, Union County, their graves being overgrown with long grass, but marked with headstones. They are the parents of twelve children :

19.   i. George, born Jan. 17, 1780 and died near Bellevue, O. February 1, 1852. While in Union County, Pa., he owned the large farm in West Buffalo township now the

home of John Watson. Mrs. Isabelle Baker, a grand-daughter, resides at Bellevue, O.

+20. ii. John, born July 21, 1781.

21. iii. Jacob, born April 18, 1783, lived and died at New Berlin, Pa., Jan. 23, 1859. They had one son, Joseph, now deceased, and a daughter, Harriet, married Jan. 16, 1851 to Col. Charles Kleckner, who served in the Civil War and now resides in Philadelphia.

22. iv. Isaac, born Feb. 27, 1785 at Orwigsburg, Pa., and died there Oct. 10, 1872. His son, Isaac, lives there now and another son, Ellwood L., resides at Lansford, Pa.

+23. v. Abraham, born Feb. 26, 1787.

24. vi. Henry, born June 27, 1789, married to Clara Wagner and died Feb. 7, 1877, without issue in Mifflinburg. He was the administrator of his father's estate. The administrator's notice is published March 12, 1841 in the New Berlin *Union Star*.

25. vii. Mary Sarah, born Aug. 27, 1791 and died Oct. 9, 1792. At another place we find the name of this one Salma Maria.

26. viii. Maria Magdalena, born December 5, 1793, married Ephraim Hackman and died June 20, 1866 in Adamsburg, Snyder County, Pa.

27. iv. Rebecca, born Feb. 21, 1796, married Thomas Crotzer and died in Mifflinburg. They left two sons, H. W. and Charles Crotzer.

+28.   x.   Samuel, born April 6, 1798.
+29.   xi.   William, born March 22, 1800.
 30.   xii.   Hannah, born July 1, 1802, never
                  married and died in Mifflinburg
                  several years ago.

10. SAMUEL³, (*Peter²*, *Gottfried¹*), born Oct. 3,
1779, married Elizabeth Hammer, who was born August
6, 1779, a member of one of the pioneer families of Berks
County, Pennsylvania. Samuel died near Grove City,
Penna. about 1859. By his wife Elizabeth Hammer, he
had twelve children as follows :

 31.   i.   Rebecca, born Sept. 22nd, 1798
                  married James Bell.
 32.   ii.   Hannah, born October 29th, 1800,
                  married Arthur McNichol.
+33.   iii.   Daniel Hammer, born October 6th,
                  1803.
34-5. iv. & v.   Twins, born October 24th, 1805,
                  died in infancy.
 36.   vi.   Elizabeth, born March 24th, 1807,
                  married Gilbert L. Lloyd.
 37.   vii.   Esther, born May 21st, 1809, mar-
                  ried Henry Crocker, residing at
                  Seneca, Kansas.
 38.   viii.   John Wesley, born December 17th,
                  1811, married Katherine Lenhart
                  of Mifflinburg.
 39.   ix.   Mary Ann, born November 17th,
                  1814, married Hugh Sharp.
 40.   x.   Isabella, born August 4th, 1817,
                  married William Herring.
 41.   xi.   Samuel Webb, born October 1st,
                  1819, married Elizabeth Auton.
 42.   xii.   James Bell, born Sept. 4th, 1823,
                  married Sarah Catherine Albin.
                  Died at Ellsworth, Kansas, Jan.
                  24, 1898.

15. ·JACOB³, (*Peter²*, *Gottfried¹*), born May 25, 1792 at Tuscarora, Pa. Married Rebecca Mains of Berks County, Pa., who was born Aug. 6, 1795 and died Sept. 30, 1854. Jacob died near Hadley, Penna. Dec. 22, 1865. By his wife Rebecca, he had eleven children:

43.	i.	Joanna, married John Hollenbaugh. Residence unknown.
44.	ii.	Temperance, born at Salem, Ohio, July 23rd, 1815, married Joseph G. Butler, Sr. Residence, Warren, Ohio.
45.	iii.	Henrietta, born ———, married Jesse Bird. Dead.
46.	iv.	Jane, born ———, married A. Loveland. Residence, Monticello, Wis.
47.	v.	Samuel M., born ———, married Sophronia Bean. Dead.
48.	vi.	James W., born Nov. 13, 1824, died February 27, 1894, married Sarah Steen.
49.	vii.	Mary Ann, born ———, married Corydon Bean. Residence, Rock Creek, Ohio.
50.	viii.	Robert L., born ———. Lives in Virginia.
—51.	ix.	Rebecca Ellen, born Feb. 15, 1832, married first David Watkins, second husband, Slathiel Pettitt. Both husbands met accidental deaths.
52.	x.	Hannah M., born ———, married Isaac Pettitt. Dead.
53.	xi.	Thomas, born ———. Died in infancy.

20. JOHN³, (*George²*, *Gottfried¹*), born July 21, 1781, moved to Mifflinburg in 1782 with his father and became one of the most prominent men of the community.

In 1820 he was the postmaster of Mifflinburg and for many years was a merchant at that place. In 1826 there was an advertisement running through the papers by John and Henry Orwig. John followed his brother George to Ohio and died in Bellevue, Sept. 25, 1844.

When John went west he located at Black Swamp, west of Fremont, Ohio, then a very heavy timbered community. Here with his boys, then quite young, they prepared a farm in the soil so black and rich. Joseph did not accompany the family west, but remained in Mifflinburg to follow his occupation, that of dentistry. While John was in Mifflinburg as a merchant, he occupied the large two and a half story brick building opposite the Deckard Hotel. Failing in business, he gave up all and with his family he emigrated in wagons to Ohio.

He was the father of nine children:

+ 54.   i.   Joseph, born Nov. 12, 1801.

55.   ii.   John, born Dec. 1803, was married by Rev. Fries in 1825 to Maria Bright. He was a doctor and died young.

56.   iii. Susanna, born July 24, 1806, married Oct. 6, 1825 to Daniel Aubel (now spelled Auble), who died at Wardsworth, Ohio, Dec. 23, 1872. Susanna died at Akron, Ohio, Nov. 21, 1887. Daniel Auble in early life was associated with "Jimmy" Cummings, as they called the genial Dry Goods Merchant in Mifflinburg. Daniel was considered a good business man and very popular, but he lost all his property, which was taken to pay claims,—made security for others. They had a family of four children, (1) James A., now living in Newberry, Pa. (2) Mary Elizabeth, married ———— Lutz,

now deceesed. Widow resides in Findley, Ohio. (3) John H. Auble, now resides in Akron, Ohio, was quite successful in business having accumulated a fortune of $75,-000 in Real Estate, Insurance and other business, but the last 15 years he lost by investments in corporations, $50,000 of it. He was a soldier in the Civil War. When his parents were poor, he bought a cozy home for them at Wadsworth, Ohio, and paid the last of the debt upon it when he returned from the war. (4) Charles H. Auble died in infancy.

57. iv. Daniel, born Jan. 5, 1809, died at the age of 60 years.

58. v. Mary Elizabeth, born April 20, 1811. She was three times a widow having married first, ———— Burton ; second, ———— Harsh; third, ———— Sherk. She raised children with each husband and died at Bellevue, Ohio, about 1885.

59. vi. Catherine, born Oct. 14, 1813, married William Roush, raised a large family and died near Clyde, Ohio, about 1883.

60. vii. Maria, born March 11, 1816, married ———————— to Thomas Roush (brother of William, the husband of Catherine.) She also raised a large family, lived and died near Clyde, Ohio, about 1883-4.

60a. viii. Henry, born Oct. 27, 1818, was married, had a family of about seven children, was in the Civil War,

		lived in Michigan and died in Kansas about 1892.
60b.	ix.	Sarah Ann, born June 2, 1821, married to Joshua Harsh, who still survives and lives near Chicago, Illinois. Sarah died about 1886.
60c.	x.	Samuel, (youngest) born Jan. 13, 1824, served in a Michigan Regiment of infantry in the Civil War and died a prisoner of war at Andersonville, having starved to death. His widow and two childred survive him.

23. ABRAHAM³, (*George*², *Gottfried*¹), born Feb. 26, 1787 in Schuylkill County, Pa., married Dec. 25, 1809 to Elizabeth Wagner and died at Orwig's Mill, in Lewis township, Union County, Pa., Dec. 16, 1852. His wife died Dec. 9, 1828 and both are buried in the old grave yard at Mifflinburg, Pa. They had six children :

+61.	i.	William W., born Dec. 25, 1810.
62.	ii.	Sarah, born Dec. 2, 1812, never married, died at Bonfield, Illinois, in 1877.
63.	iii.	Henry, born March 12, 1814, married Eliza Lebkicher of New Berlin. He died April 5, 1880 and was buried at Mifflinburg. He was a miller by trade. Four children grew to maturity, Charles H. of Millmont, Union County, Pa., Phillip S., a minister who died in York, Pa., Harvey residing at Lewisburg and Clara A., married to Horace B. Cawley, now residing in Brooklyn, N. Y.
64.	iv.	Elias, born July 15, 1816, married Rebecca Wolfe and died March 16,

1892. He had one son, Charles W., married April 16, 1871 to Alice Walter of New Berlin, now resides on the homestead in Hartleton, Pa. His mother has her home with him.

65. v. Abraham, born July 18, 1818, married Amelia Hoffman, emigrated to Illinios in 1849. He has since died and the widow with two sons and two daughters all reside in Kankakee County, Ills.

66. vi. Mary Ann, born, July 26, 1821, married to Wm. F. Hixson, moved to Illinois in 1854, died about 1888. Her husband and four children live in Bonfield, Kankakee County, Ills.

67. vii. Caroline, born Aug. 29, 1823, married John T. Smith, moved to Illinois in 1855 where her husband died about 1878-9, when she with her three sons moved to Des Moines, Iowa, where she still resides. Erastus, an attorney, practices in Denver, Col., Calvin, a doctor, and Alva, a printer, resides somewhere on the Pacific Coast.

28. SAMUEL^3, (George^2, Gottfried^1), born April 6, 1798, married Mary Meyer. Both died at Mifflinburg. Samuel died Sept. 7, 1872, aged 74 years and four months. They had five sons and three daughters:

69. i. Mary Jane, born Aug. 25, 1830, married May 24, 1853 to Jacob C. Hendricks. She died Feb. 14, 1898 at Decatur, Ills., leaving five daughters, Mamie, of Decatur; Helen, a teacher in the Chicago schools;

Mrs. E. W. Smith of Denver, Col.; Bertha, also of Denver and Mrs. G. M. Hart of Detroit. Mrs. Hendricks is survived also by her husband and two sons, Arthur of Decatur and Harry of Denver, Colo.

69.   ii.   Reuben George, born May 12, 1832, resides at 357 E. 42nd St., Chicago, Ills.

+70.   iii.   Thomas Gilbert, born June 24, 1834.

+71.   iv.   Samuel Henry, born Aug. 18, 1836.

+72.   v.   Joseph John Ray, born June 30, 1838.

73.   vi.   Benjamin Meyer, born Aug. 31, 1840; died Oct. 28, 1867 at Des Moines, Iowa. Buried at the old home in Mifflinburg Cemetery. He was Lieut. in Battery E., First Penna. Light Artillery, Army of the Potomac.

74.   vii.   Sarah Louise, born Dec. 1, 1842 and died Sept. 10, 1881 at Mifflinburg.

75.   viii.   Rebecca Hanna, born July 10, 1845, is Librarian of the Iowa Patent Office, Des Moines.

29. WILLIAM³, (George², Gottfried¹), born March 22, 1800, lived over a mile north-east of Orwig's Mill, where he owned a saw-mill and a farm, near Pleasant Grove, Lewis township, Union County, Pa. He died Feb. 25, 1869 and is buried at Mifflinburg. William's youngest son, Edward G. has a son Nelson B. Orwig, who resides at Limestoneville, Montour County, Pa. Edward G. Orwig died some years ago and his widow, Ann Rebecca, died March 20, 1898 at the home of her son, Nelson, at the age or 79 years, 11 months and 20 days. Her only daughter is Mrs. Samuel J. Reed of Mifflinburg. The funeral took place at Pleasant Grove, Union Co. Gottfried's

old Family Bible, printed in 1743, is in the hands of Nelson B. Orwig of Limestoneville, Pa., who is the son of Edward G., son of William, youngest son of George, who was the youngest son of Gottfried and Clara Orwig. In 1836 there was written in the Bible : "This Bible shall not be sold and shall remain under the name from one generation to the other. This is the wish of George and Henry Orwig." From the *Union Star*, published as New Berlin, Pa., July 3, 1840, we observe that William Orwig (now under consideration) published the administrator's notice in the Estate of Solomon Kutz, late of Hartley township, Union County, Pa. Edward G. (son of William) was born Aug. 7, 1823 and died Sept. 27, 1894 aged 71 years, 1 month and 20 days. Edward's wife, Ann R., was born March 31, 1818 and died as above stated.

33. DANIEL HAMMER⁴, (*Samuel³, Peter², Gottfried¹*), born Oct. 6, 1803, died at Bellevue, Ohio, Sept. 21, 1892 of Bright's disease. He was married Feb. 14, 1828 to Catherine Martz Hopper, who was born Feb. 21, 1811 in Montour County, Pennsylvania and died near St. Louis, Michigan, March 1885 of hydrothorax. They are the parents of eight children :

+76.   i.   John Hopper, born Feb. 23, 1829.

77.   ii.   Susanna H., born Aug. 20, 1831 at Warrior's Mark, Pa. and died Dec. 20, 1832.

78.   iii.   Samuel Abner, born March 24, 1833 at Centreville, Snyder County, Pa. Married Martha Black, born in Londerry, Ireland and died in Bellevue, O., about 1888. He lives at Bellevue, O. He has a son Dr. A. D. Orwig born Aug. 29, 1855, residing at Corner of Collingw'd Ave. and Monroe Street, Toledo, Ohio, and a son, George, a

lawyer, and a daughter, Cora, both
also residing at Toledo, O.

78.a   iv. Arthur McNichol, born Feb. 17,
1835 at Centreville, Pa., married
Mary Gilbert, is a farmer and a
pensioner residing at Mansfield, O.

79.   v. Virginia Martha, born April 21,
1838, near Mooresburg, Pa., mar-
ried Ithamar Butler Jan. 22, 185 .
and died in Chicago, April 9, 1890
They had three children, (1) Joseph
M., born Aug. 18, 1858 at New
Rochester, Ohio, married to Mima
Ashbaugh, born near Hagerstown,
Maryland. They have one child
Helen Logan Butler, born July 14,
1886. He resides at Youngstown,
Ohio, is Assistant Secretary of
Brown-Bonnell Iron Co. and has
furnished us valuable data for this
genealogy. (2) Clarice Virginia,
married to Attorney William N.
Ashbaugh was born near Niles, O.,
March 22, 1860. (3) Miles Ev-
erett, born near Niles, Ohio, Jan. 5,
1862, never married and is follow-
ing the occupation of a farmer.

80.   vi. Alexander Ross, born May 8. 1840
and died Sept. 8, 1842.

81.   vii. Nathan James, born Nov. 9, 1843
at Warren Ohio, married Sarah Al-
lis and resides at Forest Hill, Mich.
or Mansfield, O.

82.   viii. Lucy Ann, born Feb. 22, 1845 at
Price's Mills, Ohio, and died March
5, 1845.

54. JOSEPH⁴, (*John³*, *George²*, *Gottfried¹*), born
Nov. 12, 1801, was twice married, first to ————

with whom he had two daughters, one Catherine, who was married Sept. 10, 1844 by Rev. A. B. Casper of Middleburgh, Pa., to George Noecker. The family now reside in Milton, Pa. The other daughter married and went west. He was married second, Dec. 24, 1829, to Anna B. Keller, who was born June 17, 1810 and died July 4, 1874. Joseph was a successful dentist in Mifflinburg and accumulated considerable money, but most of it disappeared. He died Aug. 2, 1879. By his second marriage, he had twelve children :

83. i. Sarah Elizabeth, born Dec. 3, 1831, married Feb. 26, 1856 to William Colpetzer and died in Kansas, Jan. 18, 1881. Her husband was murdered by the Missourians, May 19, 1858. Several years before the war of the Rebellion, Mr. Colpetzer resided in Kansas, near the Missouri line. The question of Kansas being admitted as a free or a slave state was agitating the people of his state. Mr. Colpetzer was a prominent man and an able speaker and used his talents making public speeches to pursuade the people of Kansas to have a free state. Just across the line in Missouri resided a lot of slave holders who threatened to kill him if he persisted in making anti-slavery speeches. He paid no attention to their threats, but they, true to their promise, came to his house at night and demanded a peaceful surrender. He was in a position to kill them, but prefering to die innocent rather than to live with human blood stains upon his hands, he surrendered. The Mis-

sourians took him with others, and placed them in a row near Blooming Grove, Linn County, Kansas and all were shot down—martyrs to anti-slavery convictions. After the tragedy the widow and her children came back to her father's home at Mifflinburg, Pa.

84.   ii. Samuel Phineas, born May 18, 1834. Married Dec. 9, 1856 to Mary Transue. He is a retired Lutheran clergyman, having also at one time followed dentistry and is now devoting some time repairing watches, clocks and jewelry. He served in the late war and among other engagements participated in the capture of Petersburg, Va. They have three children, Annie married to Griggs Lantz, resides in Pittsburg, Pa., Milton, the operator and ticket agent at Houtzdale, Pa., married to Anna Fisher of Salem, Pa., and Sadie, married to J. Ward Diehl, now residing in Philadelphia.

85.   iii. Amanda Lucretia, born Feb. 6, 1831, married June 6, 1858 to M. O. Eilert, now residing in North Carolina. Mrs. Eilert died March 27, 1885. He was a soldier in the Civil War. They have three children, Lizzie, married to Oscar Carey of Watsontown; Charles, married to Beckie Welsh of Watsontown, Pa., is the General Manager and bookkeeper of a business in North Carolina and Nellie, married to William Schuyler of Williawsport, Pa.

86.   iv.   Andrew Jackson, born Oct. 24,
                1836, married March 18, 1861 to
                Sarah Browers and died May 16,
                1880. A daughter, Emma married
                to Eugene P. Leonard, resides with
                her husband at 1235 "L" Street,
                Lincoln, Nebr. Andrew, or "Jack,"
                as he was called, was a soldier in the
                Civil War and was shot through
                the lower jaw in front of Peters-
                burg by a sharpshooter, from the
                effects of which he died at Banner-
                ville, West Beaver township, Sny-
                der County, Pa.

87.   v.   Luncinda Ann, born April 15,
                1838, married Dec. 1, 1857 to
                Aaron Weary and died Feb. 25,
                1870. Aaron died in 1897. They
                had quite a family, among them are
                Francis, John, who resides at Lew-
                isburg, Anna (dead), Mazie and an-
                other daughter.

88.   vi.   Martha Jane, born Dec. 29, 1839,
                married March 24, 1864 to Wil-
                liam A. Orr. They have a son,
                Allen, unmarried, who is a Real
                Estate, Fire and Life Insurance
                agent at Lewistown, Mifflin Coun-
                ty, Pa., and a daughter, Grace, mar-
                ried to ———— Smith, engaged in
                the mercantile business in West
                Virginia.

89.   vii.   William Patterson, born March 13,
                1841, married in San Francisco,
                California Oct., 10, 1866 to Emma
                Dean. He served in Co. E. Fifty-
                first Penna. Regiment and later in
                the First U. S. Cavalry having

gone through the same engagements
as his brother, John, a list of which
is given elsewhere. When he was
discharged from the service in California, he secured a position in the
Custom House in San Francisco.
About 1871 he moved away up toward Washington and Oregon.
From 1871 to 1898 nothing could
be learned of him though numerous
letters were addressed to him. In
1898 word was received that he
died, 1895, in the soldiers' home in
Washington (state). In the battle
of Upperville, Va., a horse was
shot under him.

+90.   viii.   John Wesley, born Feb. 22, 1843.
91.   ix.   Malinda Delilah, born Oct. 2, 1844,
married March 7, 1867 to John
Yeatter and died June 4, 1890 at
Muskegon, Michigan. He is still
living there. They have a son,
Clarence, a daughter Florence, married and Minta, who is dead.

92.   x.   Mary Melissa, born May 15, 1846,
married Oct. 10, 1869 to Andrew
Hudgason, who resides in Lewisburg, Pa. and has five children.
Mary died Dec. 1, 1885.

93.   xi.   Joseph Clark, born Feb. 13, 1849,
is married, has a family, is a den-
tist, has accumulated some property
and resides at Herndon, Northumberland County, Pa. He has a son,
William, in the regular army, a
son, John, attending college at New
Berlin and other children.

93a.   xii.   Susan Matilda, born Feb. 28, 1852, never married, died Feb. 21, 1874.

61. WILLIAM W.[4], (*Abraham*[3], *George*[2], *Gottfried*[1]), born Dec. 25, 1810, married Susan Rishel of Centre County, Pennsylvania and died in Cleveland, Ohio, about 1887. At the age of 18 years, he entered the ministry of the Evangelical Association and became quite prominent in the church. Later he became Bishop and was editor of a German church paper, called the *Botschafter*, for a number of years. He was one of the founders of Union Seminary, now Central Pennsylvania College at New Berlin, Pa. and was its first President. This school was opened in January 1856 and our subject was Principal and Professor of Moral Science and the German language. In 1859 he resigned to devote more time to his chosen calling. By his wife, Susan, he had seven children:

94.   i.   Sarah A., married to David Harlacker, now reside at Cleveland, O.

95.   ii.   Aaron W., like his father, was a minister and also resides at Cleveland, Ohio.

96.   iii.   Thomas R., who was a member of Co. E., 142nd Regiment, Penna. Volunteers. Died 1862.

97.   iv.   Mary C., married Rev. Josiah Bowersox and died in Oregon.

98.   v.   Susan M., married Prof. Eli Hoffman, died in Cleveland, Ohio.

99.   vi.   Lizzie, married to Rev. S. L. Wiest, now residing in Harrisburg, Pa.

100.   vii.   Martha, married and died in Cleveland, Ohio.

101.   viii.   Ada, married and died in Cleveland, Ohio.

101a.   ix.   George, is a prominent physician and surgeon in Cleveland, Ohio.

70. THOMAS GILBERT[4], (*Samuel*[3], *George*[2], *Gottfried*[1]), born June 24, 1834, married Feb. 6, 1864 at Mid-

dletown, N. Y. to Mary E. Sipp. He was in the Civil
War and after his marriage his wife went with him to his
Battery at Yorktown and they began their married life in
Rebel barracks. A daughter, Mary Gilbert, was born to
them Feb. 24, 1865 and died Jan. 26, 1897. They had
an adopted daughter, Mrs. Mabel A. Sneat, who is the
mother of four children. Thomas G. is at the head of the
Iowa Patent Office established in 1870, located at 201
Fifth Street, Des Moines, Iowa. During the war he was
Captain of Battery E., First Penna. Light Artillery. During the siege of Yorktown, in 1862, while on staff duty,
he was ordered to discover a suspected rebel earthwork
near York Creek. With field glass and portfolio in hand,
he cautiously reached a wooded spot on the bank of the
creek and saw a marshy flat on the other side and a building and "Johnnies" on a rise beyond the marsh. Feeling
safe he stood up and with his glass searched the intervening
space, when three rebels arose in the marsh and fired right
at him. Closer calls in battle may have occurred, but
not realized during the excitement at such times. In the
patent office of Iowa he has built up an immense business.
He has just been nominated for Congress on the Prohibi-
tion ticket.

71.   SAMUEL HENRY[4], (Samuel[3], George[2], Gottfried[1]), born Aug. 18, 1836 at Mifflinburg, Pa., married
May 28, 1878 to Maggie Hayes of Mifflinburg. He was
educated in Mifflinburg Academy and Lewisburg University and Lewisburg Academy and spent two years at the
Yale Law School where he graduated and was admitted
to the bar of Union County, Pa., Dec. 14, 1857 where he
has since practiced. He was twice elected to the State
Legislature, first in 1864 from Union, Snyder and Juniata
district and second in 1865 from Lycoming, Union and
Snyder district. He was the Republican nominee for
Congress in 1882 and in 1884 for State Senator. During
the war he served as a private in Co. D., 28th Regiment,
(emergency men). He now resides at Lewisburg, Union
County, Pa.

72. JOSEPH JOHN RAY[4], (*Samuel[3]*, *George[2]*, *Gottfried[1]*), born June 30, 1838 at Mifflinburg, Union County, Pa., married April 18, 1865 to Jane Whiteside Stees, who was born at Oakland Mills, Perry County, Pa., Sept. 9, 1841. She was the daughter of Dr. A. C. Stees and Margaret Mitchell [Whiteside] Stees, buried at Millerstown, Perry County, Pa. Joseph R. has held numerous important public positions in Pennsylvania and Iowa. He was a captain in the Civil War and Assistant Librarian of Penna. They are the parents of six children, all born at Mifflinburg except Reuben George who was born at Harrisburg. The list is as follows :

102.	i.	Margaret Mitchell born May 18, 1866.
103.	ii.	Mary Gilbert, born Dec. 30, 1867, married Oct. 6, 1897 at Des Moines, Iowa, to Henry G. Everett.
104.	iii.	Clara Beaver, born Feb. 20, 1871.
105.	iv.	Joseph Ralph born Nov. 26, 1872, is now at Yale Law School.
106.	v.	Louisa Hayes, born Nov. 10, 1874.
107.	vi.	Reuben George, born Aug. 9, 1877.

76. JOHN HOPPER[5], (*Daniel Hammer[4]*, *Samuel[3]*, *Peter[2]*, *Gottfried[1]*), born Feb. 23, 1829 at Mooresburg, Pa. married Jan. 8, 1852 to Hannah Maria Hoover, born at Edenburg, Lawrence County, Pa., Aug. 10, 1827. They reside at Forest Hill, Michigan. They are the parents of four children :

108.	i.	Alice Emma, born Nov. 28, 1853 and died Oct. 28, 1856.
109.	ii.	Harry Ithamar, born Aug. 2, 1857 at Newport, Portage County, O., married Catherine Brack, born at Roxheim, Rhenish, Prussia, April 11, 1861. They reside at Winnetka, Illinois and have a family of four children, Sherman Brack, born at Big Rapids, Mich., April 12,

1886; Emily, born at Winnetka, June ·22, 1888; Harry Douglass, born July 2, 1891; Raymond Lloyd, born Feb. 3, 1896. Harry I. furnished some valuable data for this genealogy.

110.   iii.   John Fremont, born at Paris, Ohio, Aug. 8, 1859 and died at Forest Hill, Mich. Aug. 2, 1879.

111.   iv.   Charles Isaiah, born at Greensburg Cross Roads, Ohio, Feb. 19, 1864, married July 3, 1889 to Minnie A. White, who died at Forest Hill, Mich. March 8, 1896. Charles I. resides at Forest Hilll, Mich. By his wife, Minnie, he had three children, Harry Lee, born May 22, 1890, Lena Nell, born April 30, 1892 and Zelma, born Oct. 9, 1895, all natives of Forest Hill, Mich.

90.   JOHN WESLEY⁵, (*Joseph⁴, John³, George² Gottfried¹*), born Feb. 22, 1843 in Columbia County, Pa., married June 4, 1868 to Margaret Zellers, born, Sept. 25, 1841, in Union County, the daughter of Samuel Zellers, born May 1, 1809, died May 27, 1871 and his wife, Susanna [Stout] Zellers, born Dec. 15, 1815 and died April 22, 1877. They lived in West Buffalo township and are buried in the old cemetery at Mifflinburg, Pa. In 1849 when John was only 6 years old, his father moved to Mifflinburg where his boyhood days were spent. He was only 18 years old when the war broke out, but he was determined to go to the war and he enlisted Sept. 13, 1861 in Co. E., Fifty-first Penna. Regiment Volunteer Infantry. He was transferred to the Regular Army Sept. 26, 1862 and was assigned to the position of Bugler of Co. B., First U. S. Cavalry. He had enlisted for three years, but they offered to give a rebate of six months to those who would re-enlist for three years in the regular army. Consequent-

¹y his first term of enlistment expired Feb. 13, 1864 when he re-enlisted for three years and was finally discharged Feb. 13, 1867 at Camp McGarry, Nevada. At the close of the war, he embarked with the regulars at New Orleans, Jan. 1, 1865, for San Francisco, California and operated against the Indians in California, Nevada and Oregon. During the Civil War, he took part in the following engagements:

Burnside's Expedition.
1. Roanoke Island, N. C.
2. Newberne, N. C.
3. Camden Plains, N. C.

Army of the Potomac.
4. Second Battle of Bull Run.
5. Chantillo, Va.
6. Fredericksburg, Va., April 18, 1862.
7. South Mountain, Va., Sept. 14, 1862.
8. Antietam, Va., Sept. 17, 1862.
9. Chancellorsville, April 29, 1863.
10. Gettysburg, Pa., July 1-3, 1863.
11. Shepherdstown, Pa., July 10, 1863
12. Catholic Station, Aug. 1, 1863.
13. Battle of the Wilderness, May 8, 1864.
14. Spottsylvania, Va., May 8, 1864.
15. Sheridan's Raid, May 9-20, 1864.
16. Yellow Tavern, Va., May 12, 1864.
17. Cold Harbor, Va., June 3, 1864.
18. Travillian Station, Va., June 11, 1864.
19. Winchester, Va., July 19, 1864.
20. Manasses Gap, July 23, 1864.
21. Front Royal, Va., Aug. 16, 1864.
22. Weldon Railroad, Aug. 20, 1864.
23. Berryville, Va., Sept. 3, 1864.
24. Opequam Creek, Sept. 19, 1864.
25. Fisher's Hill, Sept. 21, 1864.
26. Wainsboro, Va., Oct. 14, 1864.
27. Cedar Creek, Oct. 19, 1864.

28.   Richmond, Va., April 3-9, 1865 which surren-
        dered to Lee.
Other Engagements.
  29.   Williamaport.
  30.   Boonsboro, July 1-12.
  31.   Falling Water.
  32.   Brandy Station.
  33.   Stanton, Va.
  34.   Upperville, Va., where he received a sabre cut
        in the head by a Rebel.

While serving as a despatch carrier for General Patrick, Provost Marshall General, he was carrying a mes-
sage from Fredericksburg to Aquia Creek over a Cordu-
roy Road, the horse stumbled and fell upon the right foot
of our subject and injured it so severely that the effects
are still noticeable.

After his discharge in 1867 he returned to his home
in Mifflinburg and studied dentistry with his brother, Samuel P. In April 1868 he located at Middleburgh, Snyder
County, Pa., the following June he was married and in
July he moved to Middleburg and practiced his profession continuously up to this time with the exception of
four years from April 1876 to April 1880 which he spent
in Watsontown, Pa. For the past 30 years he has enjoy-
ed a large and lucrative practice in his chosen profession, most of the time, having exclusive control of the
territory. In politics, he, at all times, is a Republican
and is a firm believer in the causes his party has espoused. ·

The children of John and Margaret Orwig are:
            i.   Lillian Susanna, born Jan. 11,
                 1869, married Dec. 26. 1889 to
                 Harry H. Harter of Hartleton, Pa.,
                 who was born Sept. 7, 1867. They
                 now reside at Northumberland, Pa.
                 where he is engaged in mercantile
                 pursuits. They are the parents of
                 two sons, Wilmer Orwig, born Oct.

9, 1890 and DeBriceon Orwig Harter, born Sept. 11, 1893.

ii. Miriam Ellen, born July 18, 1875,
married Oct. 22, 1896 to George
Washington Wagenseller, Editor of
the "Post," Middleburgh, Snyder
County, Pa., a full sketch of whom
is given on page 111.

iii. Infant daughter, born Feb. 23, 1883
died Feb. 26, 1883, aged 3 days.

NOTES ON ORWIG GENEALOGY.

Elizabeth Hammer, wife of Samuel Orwig, No. 10,
page 188, was a member of one of the most prominent pioneer families of Berks County, Pa., and was a most esti-
mable woman. She was a second cousin of Daniel Boone.
Samuel Orwig was about five feet, two inches in height,
spare build, of light complexion, a farmer by occupation.
His brother Jacob was about five feet, six inches in height,
stout, of light complexion, blue eyes, brown hair, mill-
wright by trade, also taught school, he having a school at
one time at Salem, Ohio. Daniel Orwig was a short, dark-
complected man, very quick on his feet and strong. His
wife was tall, large, had light eyes, of light complexion;
had quite a good education and was a beautiful writer.
Thomas Orwig, son of Samuel, son of George Orwig, of
Mifflinburg was a captain in the Union Army in the Civil
War as was his brother Joseph. Afterwards Joseph was
Secretary of the State of Iowa. Daniel Orwig's sons, John,
Arthur and Nathan were in the Union Army during the
Civil War, Nathan being with the Michigan troops who
captured Jeff Davis. Jacob's son, James, who in Civil
War on the Union side. Samuel P., John W., William P.
and Andrew J., sons of Joseph, were also in the Civil War
with the Pennsylvania Volunteers.

The Orwigs, on account of their German origin and
early environments, have been to a great extent farmers, although the younger generation now coming on are profes-

sional men, lawyers, doctors, ministers, one of them having been a bishop of the Evangelical Church at Cleveland, O., civil engineers, dentists and merchants, a very few of them working at trades.

Gottfried Orwig moved from Berks County as early as 1747 and settled at Sculp Hill, one mile south of the present town of Orwigsburg, Schuylkill Connty, Pa. They were among the very earliest settlers north of the Blue Mountains. The land upon which he settled belonged to the Iroquois Indians. The cemetery where Gottfried and Clara are buried is near the "Old Red Church" (Lutheran) near Orwigsburg, Pa. Gottfried is described as small in stature, powerfully built with strong, broad shoulders.

In 1779 George Orwig of Berks County, Pennsylvania signed a petition against calling a convention to change the Constitution of the State. This doubtless is the son of Gottfried.

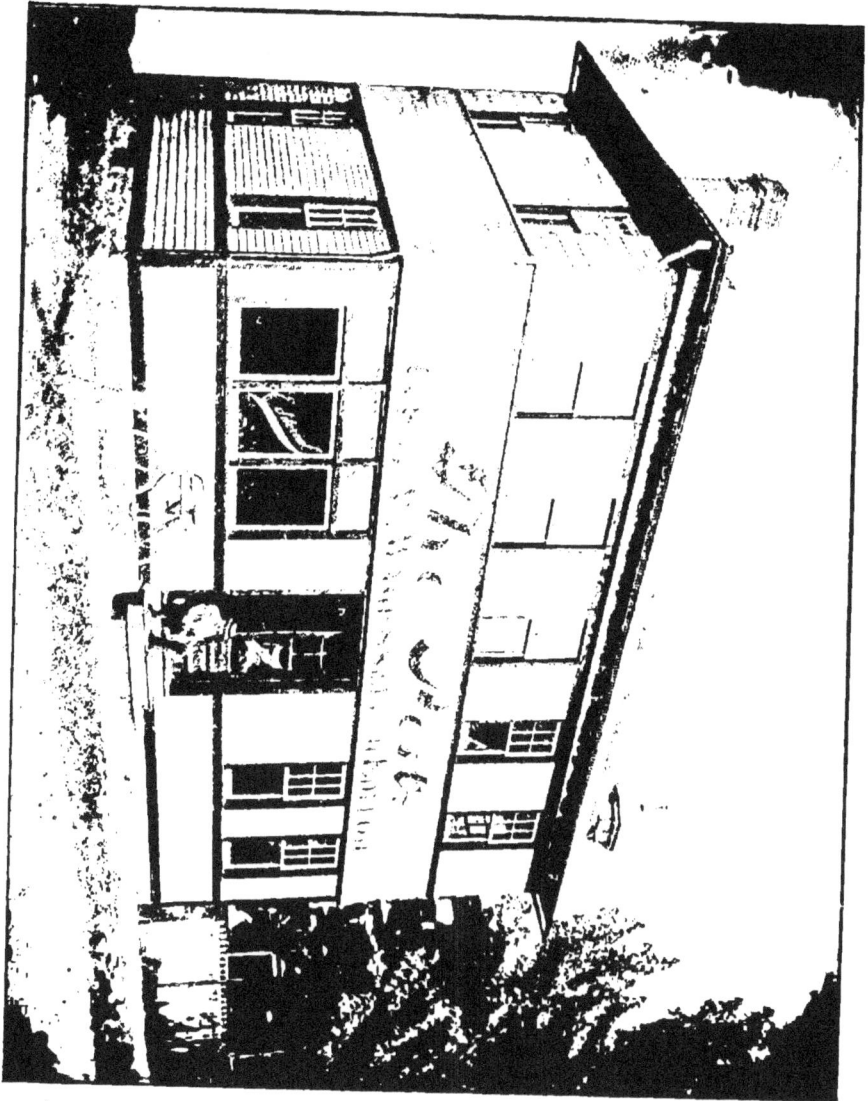

A Rambling Review.

When our common ancestor came to America and settled in Pennsylvania, nearly all was a dense forest. The foreign immigrants landed at Philadelphia and when the land was all taken up, the new-comers moved farther and farther in order to acquire a title to land that had not yet been taken up, moving to the North and West along the Schuylkill and Delaware Rivers. When Christopher Wagenseil and his wife, Anna Christina, landed, they found the land all taken up and occupied North as far as to the Perkiomen Creek. Here he selected and took up for himself 150 acres of land situate on both sides of the Perkiomen Creek not far from where the town of Pennsburg now stands. This region then was Hanover township, Philadelphia County; now it is Upper Hanover township, Montgomery County, and is situate at the extreme north-eastern corner of Montgomery County.

A conception of this region at that period, formed by us now, must necessarily be inadequate and to a large degree far from the real conditions then existing. Here in the thicket, the forest, and the wilderness, surrounded by the Indian and his tomahawk, our forefathers felled the trees, built habitations and began the cultivation of the soil. The Perkiomen Valley was rich, and its land inviting, hence it soon found an ample quantity of good industrious settlers to till the soil. The colonists came here for religious freedom and a more aggressive class of people could not be found anywhere upon the face of the globe. Six generations have tilled the very soil our ancestor till-

ed, each in its turn encountering hardships, confronting
perils, achieving triumphs, peculiar to its epoch. At the
outset came the struggle to wrest a livlihood from the vir-
gin soil. The presence of the indians, distrusted and
feared, was a source of anxiety night and day. Intercourse
with them had to be carried on with the utmost discretion.
It thrills us to contemplate the hazards to which our ancestor was subjected in this regard.   The liberty of con-
science guaranteed by William Penn brought people of
many and diverse religious convictions.   The several de-
nominations organized congregations, built churches and
school houses and it is said to the credit of most of the
early German and Dutch settlers, their church records for
completeness show a remarkable improvement over those
of the present day.   In fact the church records of to-day
too frequently are entirely a missing and an unknown
quantity.   The colonial settlers had a struggle for existence, but their church records were generally well-kept.
The War of Independence for eight years was part of their
daily life.   The battles of Brandywine and Germantown
were at their doors.   Valley Forge was only across the
Schuylkill.   The contending armies crossed and recrossed
the Perkiomen and the Shippack and marched up and
down the highways of this section of Pennsylvania.   The
inhabitants here were not only observers of these stirring
events.   Many patriotic spirits rendered heroic service
during the entire war.   Christopher, the founder of the
Wagenseller family upon this continent, was not a partici-
pant in the Revolutionary War as he died in 1762 about
13 years before the war began.   His son, John, was the
only mature male representative of the family living during the Revolutionary War.   Up to this time we have
not yet discovered authentic proof that he was in the war,
but the probabilities are that he was.   Bernard Gilbert (who
too was probably married to one of Andrew Hornetter's
daughters) was a captain in the Revolutionary War.   Jacob Shrack, the father of Martha (wife of Jacob Wagenseller p. 39) was a captain in the Revolutionary War.

History tells much of the glorious deeds of our people in those days; careful research will bring to light much more. Then followed the era of growth and expansion, of the building of bridges, turnpikes and canals, of steam and railroads and all the other evidences of civilization and modern invention.

Old Christopher, our ancestor, must have been a man of noble and positive character. He came three thousand miles braving the dangers of a tedious ocean voyage, that he might enjoy a larger manhood than was possible under the social and political conditions then existing in Europe. He was a man of high principle, chafing under the fetters which bound him in his native land. Had it been otherwise, had he been lacking in manly spirit, he would have slavishly submitted to the oppressions imposed upon him and his faithful wife, borne their degrading burdens, lived their humble lives and passed into inglorious oblivion, as did those before them, and as have done those who remained behind. The fertile lands of Pennsylvania extended to him the hand of welcome and offered to him the opportunity of a broader and a nobler life, to untrammeled effort, to religious freedom. In fact, the Perkiomen Valley needed him to cleanse the wilderness and make it yield. Of heroic stuff he was made, and no less, his wife, Anna Christina, who came up into the Perkiomen Valley.

Here was Christopher in the prime of life with the proud possession of a lovable and admirable wife. They bid farewell to many loved ones in Europe and set their hearts upon a new country and a new life. A hard struggle in Pennsylvania forests for their maintenance was a sweeter and more wholesome conception of life than the contemplation of the continuation of peasant subjection of Europe. Prompted by the high and noble characters they possessed, the way of civilization was plain and easy. Not only must the soil be tilled, but the cradle must be filled. Christopher and Anna Christina in 1760, at the making of the will had only one son and two daughters as explained elsewhere. The last will and testament of the founder of

our family, for exactness and minute detail, has no equal
scarcely in modern documents of a similar character.   The
paper was written by David Shultz, one of the witnesses.
David Shultz was a surveyor and conveyancer and the lawyer for 50 miles around in Upper Hanover township. His
residence was near the New Goshenhoppen Reformed
Church.   One night, he being away from home, an em-
ployee of his attacked and killed Mrs. Shultz in cold blood.
For many years it had been said that the miscreant had
been a slave of which Shultz had a number.   In the grave-
yard nearby a stone is erected with the epitaph: Anna
Rosina Shultzin, murdered June 14, A. D. 1750, aged 29
years.   Funeral Text, Jer. 9: 21.   Death came into our
windows," etc.

The best idea we can now get of colonial life is largely speculative.   Ah, could we but look into the homes and
hearts of the people of that period and read the history of
our paternal and maternal firesides!   Every day's detail
of their existence would make an interesting page in our
history and with what avidity would we grasp such an
opportunity!   In too many instances oblivion denies the
boon.   Very few indeed are the glimpses we get of the
life, the character and the struggles of Christopher and
his wife during the eventful period of their existence, or
even their only son, John, who moved to Providence township before the Revolutionary War began.   After the de-
feat of our armies at the battle of Brandywine and Germantown, during the dark hours when Washington had
his quarters at Valley Forge, this region was largely
drawn on for needed supplies, and its people were called
upon to contribute assistance and render important services.   The larger farmers, if not regularly connected with
the army, were impressed with their teams into the service
when occasion demanded, to transport ammunition, stores
and the wounded; of the last named, so the story goes, a
farmer hauled a load all the way from the field of Brandywine to the hospital at Bethlehem.   Providence township,
where Christopher's son, John, resided during the Revo-

lution was in imminent peril and was threatened with
danger after the battle of Germantown, so much so, that
Father Muhlenburg, then far advanced in years, sent a
portion of his family from his home in Providence to New
Hanover for safety. John[2] Wagenseil attended divine
services at the Trappe church and he, his wife and his older
children no doubt frequently heard Father Muhlenburg,
the Patriarch of the Lutheran Church in America, preach
to the interesting flock at the Providence worshiping house.
The original Trappe Church was built in 1743. The new
church was built in 1852 and was remodeled in 1878.
In 1893 the congregation celebrated the sesqui-centennial
of the Old Trappe Church and a Memorial Volume, giving the history of the church, was written by the pastor,
Rev. Ernest T. Kretschmann, Ph. D. and was published
by the congregation. Most of the family tradition of its
connection with this landmark of pioneer worship are lost,
or at least failed to reach us. Rev. Henry Anastias Geis-
senhainer, who officiated at the marriage of Peter Wagenenseller to Susanna Longaker (p. 30), was pastor of this
church from 1813 to 1821. Where he served as pastor
in 1800, when he officiated at this marriage, we have failed to learn, but it may be explained that he was a supply
preacher about this time at the Trappe. In 1796 Rev.
John Frederick Weinland was the regular paster of the
Trappe Church, but during this year his name had been
stricken from the roll of the Synod, in consequence of the
unfortunate habit of drink, which he excessively indulged.
He subsequently conquered the habit and continued as pastor up to the time of his death in the fall of 1807. It may
have been that, Dr. Henry Greissenhainer served the congregation temporarily about 1800 and hence officiated at
Peter's marriage. Rev. Frederick William Geissenhein-
er, Sr., D. D. and his son, Rev. Frederick William Geis-
senheiner, Jr., D. D., became subsequent pastors at the
old La Trappe church more commonly called the Trappe.

"Perkiomen" is one of the several Anglicized adap-
tions of "Pahkehoma," an Indian word meaning "where

cranberries grow." "Trappe" may return some day to its original name, "Trap," pure and simple ; who knows? With our forefathers "trap" was rather a favorite name for a tavern ; and both this village and a hamlet on the road to Neshaminy Falls owe their present designation to the fact that a tippler in each locality once excused himself to his wife, on returning home at an unduly late hour, saying that he had fallen into the "trap." This may look like a made-up story; but in truth, for the origin of this Montgomery county "Trap," we have the authority of H. M. Muhlenberg, who was here in the earliest days of the settlement; and in the case of the other, the episode occurred within the memory of men now living.

The descendants of the early settlers of this region, like the Wagensellers, are scattered far and wide across this great continent. From 1734 to 1790 all the Wagensellers upon this great continent resided upon the soil that is now included in Montgomery County, Pa. About 1790 the process of separation began. Of John and Margaret Wagenseller's children, John, the eldest, crossed the line over into Chester County and opened the Red Lion Hotel, Catherine married Conrad King and they went to Chester County, the old homestead being near Uwchlan, Chester County. Dr. Jacob, a son of Peter, emigrated to Selinsgrove about 1827 and his brother, William F., followed him later. Peter and his other children started the procession West in 1834, settling at Columbus, O. George, of the "Wabash," left his father's home at the Red Lion Hotel and went to Beaver County, Pa. about 1820, then to Guernsey County, Ohio and later to Crawford County, Illinois. Thus the separation began and now the name Wagenseller has entirely disappeared from the assessment books of Montgomery County, save one exception. John Wagenseller of Thorndale, Chester County, in April 1898, moved to Pottstown, Montgomery County, not more than 14 miles from where Christopher tilled the soil more than 150 years ago. Pottstown used to be, and is still fondly called by some old folks, "Potts Grove." John Potts, the miller and iron manufacturer, who laid it out in 1752, was born in Germantown in 1710 and died in 1868, "a gentleman of unblemished honor and integrity, known, beloved and lamented," said the Pennsylvania "Gazette" of that period. His elegant mansion still stands on the east side of Main Street. This country is beautiful, picturesque and fertile and for the lover of history is a prolific spot to visit. The historic Perkiomen Creek, whose placid waters flowed silently and incessantly passed our revered ancestor's home calls to mind the highest ideas of sublimity. Of all the spots in creation for Christopher Wagenseil's descendants to visit, this, without doubt, would be the most interesting. The town of Pennsburg, the one nearest to his home, is now an educational center, full of life, business and activity. We love to linger in deep thought and reverential feeling while contrasting the present Pennsburg with this region a century and a half ago, but duty calls us on to more recent family developments.

The sketches and details of the various characters that go to make up this history show to what extent our family has assisted in the development of this country. We find them in stores as clerks and proprietors, in schools as teachers, in colleges as professors, on the road as salesmen, in railroads as officers, in politics as influential individuals, in legislative halls, prominent in the medical profession, in editorial chairs, in manufacturing and industrial pursuits, conducting printing houses and more than a dozen were in the civil war fighting to maintain the Union of American States. In a thousand different ways have the various characters here represented played an important part in the progress and development of this republic.

MISCELLANEOUS DATA.

It has been necessary to introduce a brief chapter under the above heading in order to effectively use some data, that arrived too late to incorporate in the family tree where it properly belongs.

The family record of George Wagenseller Young, (pages 38-9) who resides at Newton, Kansas, shows the birth of three children, Cameron Wagenseller Young, born in Sunbury, Penna., Nov. 17, 1875; Charlotte B. Young, born July 26, 1877 in Sunbury, Penna. and Edna Washburn Young, born in Newton, Kansas, Oct. 9, 1887. Mr. young is in partnership with W. F. Kaufman in the Grocery Business. He was married to Anna F. Bourne, January 10, 1875.

PHILADELPHIA, PA., May 30th, 1898.

Data contributed by Michael Reed Minnich.

Philadelphia Co. Will Book "O" p. 136, No. 99.

Ulrich Hornecker, Will made July 3rd, 1767, probated July 29th, 1767. Leaves a wife, Magdalina. Issue, eldest son Joseph, not yet 18 years of age, son John; daughters, Margaret, Barbara, Mary Barbara. Executors, his brother John Hornecker and Peter Hillegas (evidently George Peter.) Residence, Rockhill township, Bucks County, Pa.

Administration, Bucks Co., Pa., 1782.

Administrator, George Peter Hillegas.

John Hornecker.

The late George Nyce had considerable data concerning the Hornetters. Mr. Nyce spelled the name "Hornetter" but the above contributor thinks it should be spelled "Hornecker" and considers the ancestors of John[2] Wagenseller's wife (pages 17-18) the same as his own. The date of birth of George Peter Hillegas should be 1735 instead of 1637, a typographical error on page 17.

Addanda to No. 89, page 101: Levi was married Feb. 15, 1867 to Alice Raney (or Rennie). Their first child, Anna, was born Nov. 1, 1868, married Dec. 18, 1883 to John Pavitt to whom two children are born, Mabel, Oct. 4, 1884 and Florence, April 25, 1886. Levi's second child, Wellington, was born Dec. 4, 1870, is still unmarried and resides with his mother at No. 3858 Linwood Street, Philadelphia. Levi died in 1878.

Since putting into type the article on the Schracks, pages 39-41, we learn that Martha Schrack, the wife of Jacob[3] Wagenseller, was the daughter of Captain Schrack, a soldier of the Revolutionary War. He was an officer in the command of General Wayne from the beginning to the close of the war. He was one of the men who escaped death in the Paoli Massacre. His commission and sword are still in the possession of the Schrack family. A great many of the family records of Jacob Wagenseller were destroyed in the Chambersburg fire during the war. The marriage certificate of Jacob and Martha [Schrack] Wagenseller, some naturalization papers, old deeds, administrators' and executors' papers, were sent away before the burning of the town and hence these were saved. The above we learn from a letter written by John Montgomery of Chambersburg dated June 8, 1898.

Here is the lineage of David Wagenseller, No. 98, page 58. Some discrepancy in date of birth will be noted. Which is correct, we cannot say. David was born Dec. 17, 1844, was married to Sarah Gillam, born Jan. 6, 1849 and died Oct. 9, 1894. To them we credit the birth of eight children :

1. Ella Jane, born June 10, 1869 and died July 23, 1870.
2. Nancy H., born April 1, 1871 and was married to R. H. Higgins, to whom a daughter was born June 28, 1894, another representative of the eighth generation.
3. Lillie T., born Oct. 8, 1872, died Sept. 12, 1873.
4. W. H., born Dec. 9, 1873, married Lizzie Sawyers. They have a son born March 22, 1897, another of the eighth generation.
5. Laura A., born April 6, 1877.
6. Benjamin F., born Jan. 16, 1879.
7. Orthie C., born Jan. 3, 1883.
8. Lena I., born Dec. 29, 1889.

Valentine and Catherine Hornetter, had a son George Hornetter, born Sept. 13, 1790, baptized Nov. 1790 by the pastor of New Hanover Lutheran Church. Sponsors, George Gilbert and wife, Susanna. This information may not apply to our family, but we give it here for reasons given before.

The author was in hopes of finding some trace of the graves of Christopher and Anna Christina Wagenseil before closing this volume, but a diligent search in the old Pennsburg burying ground revealed nothing. The graves may not have been marked or the bodies may have been buried on the plantation as was so often done by the people of colonial times. The church they attended is called St. Paul's. It was here also where their son, John, was baptized. It was known by the people of that vicinity as the six-cornered church, which unfortunately was destroyed by fire in 1895. A modern church was erected in 1896. This location of Pennsburg is a beautiful one. The town stands on a knoll with a valley on two sides for several miles. Hundreds of farm houses dot the valley and are in full view from the eminence of the town. The town has a population of 1200 inhabitants and has a good system of water works.

INDEX.

www.ingramcontent.com/pod-product-compliance
Lightning Source LLC
Chambersburg PA
CBHW031556280326
41928CB00049BA/772